STRATEGIC
COPILOT

ISBN: 9798309417742

Imprint: Independently published

Copyright 2024, Haig Armaghanian

All views expressed in this book are those of the author and are not intended for use as a definitive guide. This work is owned in full by the primary author, Haig Armaghanian. No part of this publication may be reproduced or transmitted in any form whatsoever without the written permission of Haig Armaghanian: haiggoesmac@mac.com

This book was produced in collaboration with Write Business Results Limited. For more information on their business book and marketing services, please visit www.writebusinessresults.com or contact the team via info@writebusinessresults.com.

STRATEGIC
COPILOT

A CEO's Guide to Changing Times

Haig Armaghanian

Acknowledgements

To my late father Hagop, thank you for being such a principled role model my whole life and teaching me the value of doing what is morally right at all times.

To my late mother Vanouhi, thank you for being the powerful matriarch of the family I was fortunate enough to be part of. You taught me the value of fighting for what you believe in.

To my sister Tania, thank you for your unconditional care and kindness. I could not have asked for a better big sister who goes above and beyond to look out for me to this day.

To my late friend Brian, thank you for being there when I most needed you, both as a friend and as a business associate. I will always remember our friendship as one that was no different to being family.

To my business partner Paul, thank you for the decades of work, friendship and the invaluable contributions you made to this book.

To my good friend and colleague William Malek who I've known for over 20 years. You are a true visionary and innovator, and working with you for so many years has shown me how prominent you are in bringing the future forward and inspiring a better future to bring to our clients. I have done my best for your many mentions in this book to do you and your work justice.

To Michael Utvich, it's been a pleasure to work with you for over 25 years, across multiple projects and industries. Your inspiration to write this book, help in conceptualising its content and setting the project alight was what made this possible.

To everyone who's worked for Haig Barrett and our clients past and present, thank you for the work and commitment to our vision. The lessons shared in this book come from work you have been a part of.

To Jon Rawding, to say the 15 years of friendship and working together have been a pleasure would be a big

Acknowledgements

understatement. It was an honour to be mentioned in your book which set the bar high when writing my own.

To all of the guests who have appeared on my podcasts, thank you for your openness with our conversations and generosity with your time. Those conversations that feature in this book add valuable context and education, which I am grateful to you for.

Lastly, to my wife Arsineh, thank you for the unwavering support not only during the writing of this book, but throughout my career and our marriage.

Strategic Copilot
A CEO's Guide to Changing Times

Dedication

To my daughters Emily and Ella, and nephews Christian and Gregory, may this book immortalise the lessons I've learned and inspire you to do great things as the next generation of our family.

Contents

Acknowledgements   I

Dedication   V

Foreword   1

Preface   5

Introduction   9

Chapter 1: Everything's Changing   15

Chapter 2: Why Transform?   29

Strategic Copilot
A CEO's Guide to Changing Times

The Executive Team   37

Chapter 3: Mindset of Successful Executives   39

Chapter 4: The Executive Mindset in Action   57

Transformation: Preparing and Staying on Track   73

Chapter 5:
Understanding and Defending Your Base   75

Chapter 6: Your Step-Out Growth Strategy   93

Chapter 7: Leadership Team   107

Chapter 8: Communicating Strategic Change   123

The Speed of Change   145

Chapter 9: Being Agile   147

Chapter 10: Resilience   157

The Art of the Long View   169

Chapter 11: Future Planning   171

Chapter 12: Strategic Foresight   185

Contents

Finding Support   205

Chapter 13:
Building Networks and Trusted Advisers   207

Business Technology & Innovation   219

Chapter 14:
Uncertainty – Obstacles to Innovation   221

Chapter 15: AI and the Digital Transformation   237

A New Approach to Work   247

Chapter 16: The Rise of the Intrapreneur   249

Chapter 17: Changing Ways of Working   269

Where Do I Start?   283

Chapter 18:
Starting Your Transformation Journey   285

Confidence in Uncertainty   301

About the Author   319

Strategic Copilot
A CEO's Guide to Changing Times

Foreword

"Hey John, what are you up to over the next few weeks," asks Haig in one of our ad-hoc, but commonly held, catch-up phone calls a decade and a half ago. "I'm doing this and that, and I'm heading over to Houston to get with the Albemarle team there," I share. A week later, Haig is flying from Los Angeles to Baton Rouge – not to have a meeting with me there, but with the sole purpose of joining me on my four-hour drive from Baton Rouge to Houston. Who does that, I thought to myself ...?

I will never forget that drive (no worries, we didn't get in a car crash). I was Haig's captive audience as he was mine. Four hours felt like 90 minutes. In an enjoyable, fully engaged random walk through many dozens of topics, Haig, in his uncannily natural way, sensed an opportunity to educate me and push me out of my comfort zone.

Strategic Copilot
A CEO's Guide to Changing Times

After ten years working together, he knew me – how I think, what I prioritise, what I'm good at and what I'm not so good at. More than just a "coach", Haig has been a partner, an extension of my capabilities, a filler against my gaps.

Me in the driver's seat, Haig is the front seat passenger ... a copilot indeed! A spot-on metaphor. What Haig taught me on the drive, ahead of the curve (for chemical industry executives at least), was the value and potential of tapping into the emerging power of the LinkedIn platform. A week or so later, I signed up to start exploiting a tool that was destined to unlock significant value for my business and career from then forward. I wouldn't have taken the step for years on my own without my copilot, for sure. Because of Haig's astuteness, what would have become a deficit, became a source of advantage and value creation for me instead. Partial credit to me for following the advice in one of the book's chapters – building a network of trusted advisers.

There were many other examples of this copilot's contributions to me and my businesses, both before and after that memorable drive as well.

I wasn't a CEO on the drive to Houston, so one of my messages to the reader is don't take the title of this book too literally. This book provides insights for executives several levels down from the CEO of an enterprise equally

Foreword

well. I have worked with Haig intimately for a quarter-century now, half as a VP-level executive, the other half as a CEO of Nasdaq-listed Codexis, Inc. If you lead teams, harness resources, aspire to make a difference in your world, CEO level or otherwise – this book will pay dividends for you.

Each chapter in this book is relevant, informative and actionable. But after your first read, go back and target your application of the book with an eye on your gaps as a leader/CEO. Take the time to reflect objectively on the question. Then use this book to sharpen how to address those – find that copilot advice to help fill those gaps and extend your impact.

For me, strategic thinking, plus managing uncertainty and ambiguity with agility, always came naturally. I'm honoured to have been highlighted by Haig in those chapters in this book. But my gaps – honestly earlier in my career, my blind spots – have always focused around my deprioritising time spent externally, plus truly maximising the productivity of my leadership team. I benefited by working directly with Haig over the years on these topics. That took me years and not a trivial amount of consultancy fees. But you have the benefit of this book of Haig's wisdom to tap into rapidly and inexpensively. Lucky you.

Strategic Copilot
A CEO's Guide to Changing Times

But also, lucky me. Over my 35+ years as a business leader, and the many people I have worked with over that time, it is unfortunately true that long-lasting friendships don't often emerge from the business world. And interestingly, friendships from within the company translate even less. On the contrary, many of my deepest long-term friendships have emerged from those few external advisory partners I've worked with across my many career chapters. You, my friend Haig, are among the rarified top of that list. As I have now embarked on my semi-retired chapter of life, launching and building my new advisory practice, Organicols LLC, I look to emulate you and deliver for others what you've so instinctively done for me. Thanks so much, Haig.

Reader – dive in, absorb the advice and structured approaches throughout this fine book. And take the step to seek and reap the benefits of your own external copilot relationship. Enjoy!

John Nicols
CEO and Owner of Organicols, LLC

Preface

I will always have fond memories of my mother telling me stories of her father (my grandfather), Artin, and his approaches to business and life.

Artin Cherchian arrived in Cyprus in the early 20th century. He did not plan to move to Cyprus, his only plan was to escape dangers in his homeland, and as such he boarded a boat to an unknown destination.

Like many Armenians in his position, he had very little to start a new life in unknown territory. He was, however, equipped with humanity, a sense of community and a strong moral compass.

Artin began a confectionery business by travelling for miles to a church, where he would set up a stand full of sweets called "helva" and give them away for free. They were popular, and soon Artin started selling them outside the church until he could afford to set up his own shop.

His shop was different from a typical sweet shop. As well as manufacturing and selling helva, part of the shop was an apothecary. People in the community would come in to tell him their ailments and he would give away herbal remedies for free.

Artin became known as someone who would provide quality helva, help people for free and offer those needing work jobs in the shop. The value he provided built trust with his customers and helped his business grow. He did not give generously to build a strong business reputation, however. He did so because he believed in doing the right thing, and he chose to express his values in all areas of his life, including business.

I can verify through my own career that a century later the core principles of business are the same. Providing value and understanding humanity is the best way to succeed in having a thriving business as well as a fulfilling life.

The following book is full of lessons, principles and tools I have learned and used myself in decades of business as a consultant.

Preface

It is written in the legacy of my family who taught me to always do the right thing and express my values in all areas of my life.

For anyone reading, thank you. The support is never taken for granted and I have done my very best for readers to gain as much value as possible.

Strategic Copilot
A CEO's Guide to Changing Times

Introduction

Since the turn of the 21st century the world has changed dramatically. As I write this in 2024, it seems as though the rate of change has accelerated considerably. Unexpected, highly disruptive global events are happening with greater frequency and planning ahead is becoming increasingly challenging.

For you as a CEO, this presents new and unique challenges. All of a sudden you have found yourself in a business landscape that you may not know how to navigate. It is one where the agile survive. Those who cannot pivot quickly find that they lose ground and market share to their more nimble competitors. For large organisations in particular, it can be difficult to know how to find a way through.

Strategic Copilot
A CEO's Guide to Changing Times

If you head up a large organisation in a sector such as biotech, pharma, oil and gas, water or chemical engineering, rapid adaptation becomes even more challenging due to the nature of the sector in which you operate. But that does not mean rapid adaptation isn't possible.

A new way of doing business

What we are entering is a new era of doing business, one where many of the old rules are being cast aside. The ways in which businesses accelerate their growth are changing. If you want your organisation to still be leading the way in ten or even five years' time, you need to adapt your approach.

Having been a business consultant for over 25 years, I have had the unique opportunity to observe how some of the world's most successful companies pivot, innovate and grow. I have supported some of those transformations, helping CEOs and their executive teams to find the right strategy for their organisation.

I have also been lucky enough to build a network with many more executives from organisations all over the world, who have been kind enough to share their insights and stories with me on my podcasts – *Between the Lines with Haig*, *Other Side of the Business Card* and *The*

Board Perspective. You'll hear some of these insights as you move through the coming chapters, and you'll learn more about the stories behind these highly successful CEOs and executives.

I've written this book to share my knowledge around strategic change and transformation, because I increasingly see CEOs and executive teams struggling to adapt to the new ways of working that have been thrust upon us. You'll notice that I have broken the chapters down by theme, with each covering an area that I have learnt is essential for building an adaptable organisation that can stand the test of time and weather storms of all kinds.

There are exercises and tools throughout this book that you can use to get started on your own transformation journey. But one thing I cannot stress enough is the value of seeking external support on this journey. The role of consultants is often misunderstood, so I also want to demystify the processes I use with my clients so that you can see the value in having this external perspective.

For the changemakers

This book is for CEOs who are not afraid to push the destruct button, tear up their strategy and pivot if they need to. I can already tell that you fall into this camp because you've picked up this book. You are not content to do the same things you always have and follow the status quo. You are comfortable being challenged. You are not scared of what lies ahead. However, you may be uncertain about what the future holds.

Uncertainty is dangerous because it can cause even the most decisive of leaders to hesitate for a fraction too long. By its very nature, change brings uncertainty. What I hope to do through this book is help you to develop confidence even in the face of uncertainty.

Before we dive into the how, let's first explore the landscape in which we find ourselves following the Covid-19 pandemic and various other shocks to the global economy. We need to understand where we are in order to chart a path to a different future. We'll also cover the blocks to transformation to better understand why so many organisations still look to the past instead of creating their futures.

Once we have a strong idea of why transformation is necessary, I'll take you through the various elements you need to master for a successful transformation journey:

Introduction

In the final chapter and conclusion, you will find a blueprint to help you start your own business transformation, armed with the tools and knowledge you need to stack the likelihood of success in your favour.

You know you want to lead change, that's why you picked up this book. So, let's start by taking a deep dive into the business landscape of the 2020s, to better understand and make the case for business transformation.

Strategic Copilot
A CEO's Guide to Changing Times

Chapter 1

Everything's Changing

None of the executives I speak to or work with deny that the world is undergoing a period of significant change. The Covid-19 pandemic might have provided a dramatic and sudden shift in the way in which we operate businesses and live our lives, but change was already happening, and quickly, before the pandemic hit in 2020.

One of my favourite quotes from Peter Drucker is: "The greatest danger in times of turbulence is not the turbulence. It is to act with yesterday's logic".[1] In other words, change is not what presents the danger. Rather, attempting to deal with change using outdated tools and strategies is the greatest danger to your organisation. Believing that what worked yesterday will continue to

---

1 Drucker, P.F. (1959) *Landmarks of Tomorrow*.

work tomorrow is a fallacy. In many cases, what seems to work today may well not work tomorrow.

Therefore, as a business leader, you need to become comfortable with change, no matter what form it takes. This is the most crucial skill any CEO can have, and it is the one that will single out businesses that succeed from those that fail.

Remaining relevant

CEOs who constantly innovate and seek new ways of approaching their businesses will ensure that they remain relevant and at the forefront of their industries in a rapidly shifting world. What adaptation and innovation looks like for you and your organisation will depend on the industry in which you work.

One person who knows what it's like to deal with constant change is Bindiya Vakil, CEO and co-founder of Resilinc. When I spoke to her on the *Other Side of the Business Card* podcast, she explained that in the world of supply chain sourcing and procurement, which is her speciality, you have to become adept at dealing with change.

Chapter 1:
Everything's Changing

Spotlight on Bindiya Vakil

Role: CEO and co-founder, Resilinc

Tenure: May 2010–present

Biggest strengths: Ability to evaluate supply chains and help global organisations transform the way they approach supply chain visibility and risk.

Achievements: Starting and growing a successful business, Resilinc, which has become a world leader for supply chain visibility, resiliency intelligence and analytics.

"Procurement seems like it's in a perennial state of disruption. One day you're dealing with a factory fire. Then there's a hurricane halfway around the world. Then you've got a port strike

> or a labour issue. During my procurement career, I always felt like we were chasing shortages or at the mercy of suppliers and events, on a near-constant level. Always being very reactive was very uncomfortable for me. I went to MIT to study supply chain and one of my professors there – Yossi Sheffi – was writing a book called *The Resilient Enterprise*, which was about how companies could proactively manage their supply chains. That made me really excited, because it showed me there might be a better way." [2]

After completing her master's, Bindiya went to work for Cisco where she joined a group focused on supply chain risk management. At this time, the company was dealing with the fallout from Hurricane Katrina. Five years and a lot of learning later, Bindiya left her corporate role to co-found Resilinc in 2010. Like all of us, she found herself navigating the Covid-19 pandemic ten years later, and helping her clients do the same.

> "The pandemic, I would say, is *the* black swan of black swan events. Of course prior to this we'd had earthquakes, floods, tsunamis, the Icelandic volcano eruption, multiple bankruptcies

---

2 *Other Side of the Business Card*, Bindiya Vakil (July 2021). Available at: https://www.haigbarrettpartners.com/the-other-side-of-the-business-card/episode/2b056833/transforming-supply-chain-risk-management-with-bindiya-vakil.

Chapter 1:
Everything's Changing

and even other pandemics like swine flu. But these were all still sporadic events that affected some companies and not others. The [Covid-19] pandemic spared no one. Every human on the planet today has seen supply chain disruption and personally we have all been affected by it. We have seen people lose their lives and their livelihoods, in many cases because the supply chain failed."

The term "black swan event" originated in Nassim Taleb's book of the same name, in which he described the impact that rare and unpredictable outlier events have on businesses.[3] These are scenarios that people haven't planned for. In the years since the book's publication, the term has caught on. Some might say that it's been overused in the wake of the Covid-19 pandemic, but the fundamental premise behind Taleb's theory on black swan events remains true: the future is now based on a level of uncertainty that traditional organisations aren't designed for.

I have spoken with many CEOs who used to produce five-year strategic plans, often with the support of external consultants, but by year two their plan has already changed so much that it is no longer relevant.

---

3   Taleb, N.N. (2007) *The Black Swan: The Impact of the Highly Improbable*. Random House.

Strategic Copilot
A CEO's Guide to Changing Times

My philosophy, therefore, is not to support executives to come up with five-year plans that can withstand the uncertainty, but instead to work with executive teams to develop their mindsets so that they are able to change their plan and work within that uncertainty.

In many cases, this means finding that team and organisation's "true north", which can guide them in their decision-making without making them completely reliant on certain predicted outcomes being true. The biggest change that these executives need to make to the way they operate is accepting that they don't have all the answers and developing a much more agile approach to their quarterly strategy meetings. The key is to find confidence in the uncertainty.

For a CEO, this requires a new approach to not only formulating strategy, but also to presenting it to the Board. Gone are the days when you could present a five-year strategic plan to your Board and have it signed off. With so many elements changing so quickly, CEOs need to be more agile, and they need to bring their Boards with them on that journey.

As Bindiya explained, businesses also need to consider how they can balance making cost savings, becoming lean and reducing inventory while still ensuring access to everything they need in order to operate.

Chapter 1:
Everything's Changing

"Toyota is a company that we often think of as the global standard for a lean business, but that fails to account for how Toyota has removed some of the risk from its supply chain. The semiconductor shortage [in 2021 and 2022] cost automakers billions. In 2021, Ford announced it expected the shortage to lower its earnings by $2.5 billion,[4] while at the same time Toyota was saying that it didn't expect the semiconductor shortage to affect its business. How could a company we all consider to be so lean not be affected by the supply chain disruption every other automotive company was facing?

An article for Bloomberg explained that Toyota had identified the 1,500 components that had the highest impact on its revenue – many of which were semiconductors – and had a robust supply chain, mapping, monitoring and inventory management capability.[5] This meant they had stockpiled to some extent, which allowed them to continue operating as normal for four months

---

4   Team, T. (2021) "Ford Stock Vulnerable to Semiconductor Chip Shortage?," *Forbes*, 29 June. Available at: https://www.forbes.com/sites/greatspeculations/2021/06/04/ford-stock-vulnerable-to-semiconductor-chip-shortage/.

5   Bloomberg (2021) "How Toyota Steered Clear of the Chip Shortage Mess," *Bloomberg*, 7 April. Available at: https://www.bloomberg.com/news/articles/2021-04-07/how-toyota-s-supply-chain-helped-it-weather-the-chip-shortage

longer than any of their competitors. Toyota was eventually impacted, but this supply chain disruption stemmed from the black swan of black swan events, and the company successfully mitigated that for a time by focusing on risk reduction."

Adaptability and resilience: the new business critical

One of the things I've noticed in the years since 2020 and the Covid-19 pandemic is that there is more freedom to accept failure among the executives my team and myself work with. A decade ago, there was a sense among executives that if they did something wrong it would be the end of their career. They felt as though they should know everything and have all the answers.

As I write this, however, we haven't seen business as usual for a number of years. In the UK there was Brexit, then globally we've had the pandemic and wars in Ukraine and the Middle East. This has led to a shift in perspective and many of the talented younger generation who are coming through are used to working in an environment where nothing is certain. They can't predict what will happen the following year in terms of supply chain, raw materials, available services, which countries goods can be shipped through, and so on.

Chapter 1:
Everything's Changing

William Malek, an executive facilitator who has supported some of the world's largest companies with their transformations, understands this uncertainty better than most. He advocates for systemic transformation to ensure organisations are set up for much more rapid, agile decision-making.

Spotlight on William Malek

Role: Chief Strategy Officer for SEAsia Rendanheyi Research Center, a collaboration with Haier Model Institute (HMI); Co-Founder and CEO, Strategy2Reality LLC: advised, facilitated and trained organisations in aligning strategic initiatives with execution capabilities.

Tenure: September 2020–present; 2007–present

Biggest strengths: Leadership development. William's core strength lies in his ability to mentor and

> elevate mid-to-senior level leaders, enabling them to navigate and drive strategic outcomes even in highly uncertain environments. He focuses on cultivating autonomy within enterprises, empowering leaders to independently innovate, execute, and scale their initiatives. This approach ensures that leaders are not only prepared to meet present challenges but are also equipped to foster a forward-thinking, future-fit, growth-oriented culture.
>
> **Achievements:** Developed and ran a management programme at Stanford University.

There is a greater need than ever before for what William terms "strategic foresight". Everything is changing at a much faster pace than it ever has, and strategic foresight means you have a stronger set of analysts working with you who can help you to understand strong and weak signals in the market, and have a good grasp of what the leading indicators for change or disrutption are.

> "I think today's challenge is probably an order of magnitude greater than we have ever seen. It's radical and we are in a whole different scenario to what we faced in 2008.
>
> To a large degree, the notion of prediction has changed. When you look at other possible

Chapter 1:
Everything's Changing

disruptors, shifts or changes, some will be natural, and some will be imposed by external events. You have to change the way you look at planning and sensing the future that you're trying to execute towards.

In my world, where execution used to be the second step of strategy, the execution piece is now even more critical because I need to be doing things while I'm learning about what future is emerging. You learn very fast by're almost experimenting. You cannot plan. You have to be doing to actually learn what you should do differently by testing ideas. I think the Covid environment has provided a great big innovation lab globally, because you've got to rethink everything. We've got to work out how we can do this faster, better, cheaper and so forth" [6]

I have been working with companies for 30 years and many of them have always assumed that once they have put together their plan, they don't need a great deal of strategic foresight beyond that. However, in today's world, that has changed. Organisations that currently lack this strategic foresight might be wondering how to introduce

---

[6] *Between the Lines with Haig*, William Malek (January 2021). Available at: https://www.haigbarrettpartners.com/between-the-lines-with-haig/episode/27351209/episode-1-william-malek.

it and the key is to become a flatter organisation that can operate with strong relationships between departments or other nodes in an ecosystem.

One of the most important relationships is between marketing and operations, because it's essential for any business to understand the voice of the customer. Organisations that want to get ahead and stay ahead need to employ people who know how to stay connected to their customers and who are going to nurture those relationships. The days of simply taking orders and doing the minimum of relationship building are over.

The challenge is that the majority of large corporations are designed around keeping the organisation running with "business as usual". In many cases their budgets are simply based on the previous year. Too many of these organisations are resisting change because they don't see the need to change until the problems they face are bigger than the obstacles immediately in front of them.

However, there are signs that this way of working cannot continue. The Covid-19 pandemic is a good example of where companies that were more agile were rewarded, while those that clung on to "business as usual" suffered.

How future fit is your organisation?

Chapter 1:
Everything's Changing

To be future fit, firstly you need a very strong leader who can change the mindset of the leadership team. In some cases, you'll only be able to change the mindset of two-thirds of the leadership team and you'll receive pushback from the remaining third. In this instance, a good leader is able to balance those two positions without turning the table upside down. They are able to push for change at the right rate and they have the strength to get rid of the people who will not adapt to this new way of working.

But leaders need to be able to adapt to the future without becoming rigidly attached to an idea of what that future might look like. As William Malek explained when we spoke on the *Between the Lines with Haig* podcast, prediction is a fool's game but that doesn't mean you can't prepare for the future and build resilience.

> "You have to pay attention in your context, where you live, where you work and where you have influence. You need the ability to see beyond what is just in front of you. The capacity to become more aware will help you become more resilient and give you more confidence in the choices you make to move forward in a world that seems to be unstable and not necessarily capable of being predicted.

You need to reach a place where you can at least understand the variables and not react to them negatively. You've got to become more resilient. My hope for people is that we don't get so freaked out that we become driven by fear, because if we're driven by fear the outcomes aren't going to be pretty. The outcomes look very different when they're driven by positive, proactive change and being able to look at this as an opportunity to reframe our lives, our careers and our communities.

Covid-19 has opened the door for us to experiment in a whole new way. The door is open for us to make a change."

But what does this experimentation look like in practice? And how can you, as a leader, step through this open door that leads to change on a fundamental level?

Chapter 2

Why Transform?

In 2007, biochemicals company Codexis announced a collaboration with Shell to develop biofuels.[7] Shell invested significant sums in Codexis and its research, and the research agreement continued until 2012.[8] However, at this time the global appetite for biofuels and the research surrounding them collapsed, leaving Codexis with a dilemma – should they stick with their focus on biofuels or expand into other areas?

---

7   Euro-Énergie (2009) "Shell and Codexis Deepen Collaboration to Speed Arrival of Next Generation Biofuel," 11 March. Available at: https://www.euro-energie.com/shell-and-codexis-deepen-collaboration-to-speed-arrival-of-next-generation-biofuel-n-1170.

8   Renewables Now (2012) "Codexis to Cut 133 Jobs Upon Ending Research Agreement with Shell," 4 Sept. Available at: https://renewablesnow.com/news/codexis-to-cut-133-jobs-upon-ending-research-agreement-with-shell-300324/

During this period, John Nicols was the company's CEO. He and I had worked together previously and so he brought myself and my team in to help him make this decision about the company's future. He knew that Codexis needed to rethink its strategy, but the challenge was that he didn't have anyone with whom he could openly discuss his views in the company.

In fact, many people within the business were actively fighting against a pivot away from biofuels, because this was where their expertise lay. Therefore, it was in their interests for the focus on biofuels to continue, as that provided job security. But John could see that continuing with biofuels research may not be feasible for the company in the long term. What he needed was a team who he could talk to openly about other possibilities, so that he could make an informed decision on which direction to take the company in.

The main technology Codexis had focused on in the biofuels race was developing enzymes to convert biomass into new types of biofuels. But enzymes can be used in many different fields.

Our process enabled Codexis to quickly identify the biopharma market as another opportunity for them to use this technology.

Chapter 2:
Why Transform?

This was where my team proved invaluable, because we were able to quickly bring in experts in very specific fields. While John's internal team knew the biofuels market inside out, they weren't qualified to look at the biopharma or biotech industries.

We carried out a lot of market analysis using specialist analysts who knew both the biofuels and biopharma markets well. In doing so, we helped John gain confidence in the other business models open to Codexis and were able to support him in presenting these findings to the Board and the other executives.

We took John from facing a big dilemma and not knowing what to do, to having clarity over the direction the business needed to move in, and getting buy-in for the change from his peers and the company's Board. John pivoted the whole business. It was a process that took many months and resulted in two-thirds of the vice-presidents and senior vice-presidents in the organisation stepping down.

There were many conversations with shareholders, investors and current customers during this period to ensure everyone's voices were heard and that the decision was inclusive. More than ten years on, it's clear this was the right decision. Not only does Codexis continue to serve the biopharma industry, but its technology has enabled the company to develop its own therapeutic products. This has helped the organisation to evolve still further.

John's story is a great example of why transforming your organisation is worthwhile, as long as this transformation is based on data and careful analysis of the situation. But there are many stories of companies that fail to take advantage of such opportunities to pivot.

Why do companies resist transformation?

There are many reasons why companies resist transformation, but often it comes down to underestimating two main areas:

1. The financial outlay of hiring the right consultant or hiring new people to get the result they want in the market they want to move into.

2. How good their technology is and how transferable it is to a market that could be 10–20 times the size of the one in which they currently operate.

One German company I worked with underestimated in both of these areas. The business wanted to spend a quarter of what was needed to move into the new market, and was being slow to make the shift. While this is a generalisation, more often than not European companies

Chapter 2:
Why Transform?

are more risk-averse than their US counterparts, which can mean they miss out on opportunities. Instead of taking the leap, they hold back. This allows another business to fill that niche.

Hope is not a strategy

Many businesses want to expand into new markets and want to grow, but they aren't prepared to do what's necessary to get there. All too often we see low numbers attached to go-to market strategies to make the shift seem more affordable when it's presented to the Board or the next layer of management, but this underestimates the size of the task. As a result, the expansion and growth they are seeking doesn't occur.

Instead, they need to spend more to develop complete plans and execute them. If more businesses were prepared to approach expansion and growth strategies in this way, they would see greater success.

As William Malek put it wonderfully when we spoke on *The Board Perspective*, in 2021:

> "When we hear the word 'future' we think it's out there. We think that if we plan something today, hopefully in the future we will see an outcome of

> A, B and C. But the reality is, what we do today is the biggest predictor of our future."[9]

There is no question that businesses need to transform their ways of working, and we'll explore throughout the rest of this book how you can do that in an ever-changing world. But I'd like to close this chapter with some of William's thoughts on planning and, more specifically, how we need to move away from planning and focus on taking action.

> "We have to let go of planning. If you look at organisations that have to move fast, their strategy emerges as a result of the people who are making decisions about what needs to happen. To let go of planning, you need to get your organisation engaged to really figure out what needs to maintain paying customers. You have to ask, how do you manage your liquidity and cashflow to grow the business?.
>
> The challenge is to get closer to the people who are engaged in the actual work and, more importantly, customer focused. This means those who are talking to customers and looking at customer data. In times of flux and change, these are the people

---

9   Haig Barrett Partners (2021) *Why Transform – The Board Perspective: Episode 1 with William Malek.* Available at: https://www.youtube.com/watch?v=W1-XCvv1nHQ.

Chapter 2:
Why Transform?

who need to be engaged in helping organisations decide what to do, not five people on a Board who are not in the running of the business ...

By flattening the organisational structure, you begin to see a collective intelligence and an emergence of a discussion that is far more powerful than three or four people sitting on a Board trying to guess what to do. Use your employees. Use your people who are in your system to inform you about what is happening today, and how they see the future."

That's not to say that the Board isn't important and doesn't have a role in future-fit organisations. It certainly does. But Boards, and businesses, that thrive will be the ones that create systems that allow people within the organisation to operate with a greater degree of autonomy. This means those closest to customers can use their intimate knowledge of what people actually need to deliver growth for the business, while the Board can take a more strategic perspective on the organisation and its trajectory.

Strategic Copilot
A CEO's Guide to Changing Times

To access additional resources around the theme of change management, scan the following QR code:

The Executive Team

The world has undergone seismic shifts in the way in which businesses operate. It's clear that the old ways of working simply don't deliver results any longer. This presents a challenge to executive teams, and a challenge for any CEO who is building an executive team.

What qualities and traits do executives need to thrive within an environment of near-constant uncertainty? How can you find people who embody those traits and bring them to your organisation? How has an executive's role, and therefore a CEO's role, changed? What mindset do you need to adopt in order to lead your organisation now and into the future?

All of these are valid questions, and ones that many CEOs and Boards are asking themselves. In the next two chapters, we'll explore the mindset of successful executives and see how this translates into tangible business benefits.

Chapter 3

Mindset of Successful Executives

As a leader, you will play different roles at different times. These roles have shifted over the years. McKinsey has identified four key roles that leaders in 21st-century organisations need to embody: visionary, architect, coach and catalyst.[10]

The visionary is exactly what you would expect – setting a clear mission and vision for the future that everyone can get behind. When you play the role of the architect, you

---

[10] Lure, M. and Tegelberg, L. (2019) "The New Roles of Leaders in 21st Century Organizations," *McKinsey & Company*. Available at: https://www.mckinsey.com/capabilities/people-and-organizational-performance/our-insights/the-organization-blog/the-new-roles-of-leaders-in-21st-century-organizations.

take the lead on designing an empowered and sustainable organisation. This is important when planning and strategising for an uncertain future, as I'll discuss later.

Being a coach means that you encourage those on your teams to develop their own capabilities and level up alongside the organisation. You also create an environment where people feel free to experiment. Finally, as a catalyst, you remove roadblocks to your teams' progress, encourage people to build connections with one another and the organisation's mission, and create a welcoming and inclusive environment.

Successful executives are able to move between these different roles and know which one to adopt when. Of course, some people will be naturally suited to being a visionary, while others may find coaching or being an architect comes more easily. This highlights the value of a strong and balanced executive team, where all of these roles are expressed.

But one thing that all great leaders have in common, regardless of which role they are currently embodying, is a growth mindset.

Chapter 3:
Mindset of Successful Executives

What makes a growth mindset?

Throughout my career, I have always worked with clients and companies that embody a growth mindset. What's interesting about people and companies with a growth mindset is that they're a lot more protected against failure than organisations that have a fixed mindset. Among the traits of those with a growth mindset are being willing to take risks, albeit calculated ones, and knowing how to deal with an inherited team.

In many cases, teams aren't perfect, so it's essential to be able to adjust the team so they can support the strategy you want. Ideally, you also want to upskill the team so that you have the knowledge and skills you need to execute effectively. This means you need to be able to sell to the CEO (assuming you're not in this position) and the Board what you're missing in that team to have a collective growth mindset.

You also need to be what I term "anti-failure". What I mean by that is you can accept failure for what it is and learn from it to pivot, all while doing what you can to minimise the chances of failure in the first place.

I had one client in the Middle East who wanted to build up their thought leadership and connect with their clients, so they decided to run free seminars. They booked nice hotels and invited people who they thought would be interested. They expected 50–60 people would turn up for these free events. Failure in this instance would have seen no one turning up for their events, and my client having wasted their time on putting together the curriculum and content. But they took a calculated risk and embraced the anti-failure mindset.

As it turned out, they had so many people coming to their events – close to 100 in many cases – that they decided to charge people to attend. Now this client speaks to audiences of over 500 people in locations all over the Middle East. Theirs is a success story, but it could easily have been different. Had this approach not been right for their market, their customers or their products, they would have needed to rethink their strategy.

They were willing to rethink their strategy if necessary. But before they did so, they needed to act. They needed to get closer to their customers and find out what they actually wanted. They did that through these events and discovered that their approach worked.

Another important element of a growth mindset is understanding the importance of "unlearning", in the sense that you are able to unlearn the way things were done before and view every part of your organisation through a fresh pair of eyes.

Chapter 3:

Mindset of Successful Executives

The need to influence

John Maxwell once said: "He who thinks he leads, but has no followers, is only taking a walk."[11] This speaks to the need to be able to influence others and work closely with Boards and people across different teams in the business to bring them to the right place.

In my experience of working with leaders in the corporate world, I would say that around 20 per cent of leaders can move the needle. In these organisations, leaders that succeed need to understand politics and they need to be able to sell their ideas. In other words, they are not only able to be a visionary, but they have the ability to convince others to buy into their vision.

To generate a high level of buy-in among your teams, you need to have a very clear story about what you want to do, and to be able to articulate that in such a way that you can get others to emotionally buy into your narrative. Brian O'Keefe, who you'll hear more from later in the book, has a standardised framework for how to frame a problem that he teaches 20 per cent of leaders in the organisations he works with. The idea being that this enables you to quickly frame an initiative or even a request for more money, and communicate

---

11   Maxwell, J. (2007) *Ultimate Leadership: Maximize Your Potential and Empower Your Team*. Thomas Nelson.

it to generate buy-in. This is all about selling business concepts internally. To succeed in leadership, you need to be able to sell across divisions, and to do so upwards and downwards.

One of my specialist abilities is being able to see multiple perspectives within an organisation. This allows me to offer my clients suggestions of different ways in which to present the same problem to different people or divisions. These different perspectives also help the CEOs I work with to make their plans more bulletproof.

This is where I see the value of consultants like myself. We are people who can help to fill gaps in your organisation because you're growing too fast, for example, and you don't have the resources you need to manage that growth. Think about a baby who has what is often termed "baby fat", then they go through a growth spurt and all of that fat is used up. Many of the organisations I support don't have the "fat" to support a growth spurt, but through my network of worldwide consultants, I have the "fat" they need to fill in the gaps as they grow.

Myself and my team can even help our clients hire the right people into their businesses by helping them to find the right-fit people who understand what they're trying to build, and have the experience and knowledge to support that strategy.

Chapter 3:
Mindset of Successful Executives

We can also help you to unlearn what you think you know. Doing so can allow you to see pathways that may have been hidden before, but that have the potential to lead to significant growth.

Developing a demolition mindset

When you have a demolition mindset, you're willing to break apart everything you have in your organisation and see what you've got in terms of your leadership team and what they're capable of. This concept comes out of re-engineering, which involves stripping out the waste and restructuring. In the past, you were able to do this with some level of knowledge about what products were coming into the market and which ones were leaving it.

However, today's leaders have to not only learn to rebuild with what they have, but also have to rebuild with a view to doing so to survive and thrive in an uncertain future. This is when being the architect is important. You have to consider what you're building for that you don't know about, which is a bit more like going on a Christopher Columbus expedition than taking a boat down the River Thames. You have to prepare for a different world and you have to accept that you likely won't have all the right people in your team to do so effectively.

One option in this instance is to bring in strategic help like myself, which I would estimate around one-third of leaders do. The other option is to lay people off and find the right people to hire in their place to allow you to build the organisation for the future you want to see. Which of these options is right for you will depend on your organisation's specific circumstances and future aspirations.

The value of strategic thinking

When you reach the executive level in an organisation, it is essential that you set aside time for strategic thinking, both as an individual and as a leadership team. Ideally, you would take everyone out of the office environment for a few days, because this gives you and your team an opportunity to focus on the company itself with no distractions, either professional or personal.

In many organisations, it seems to me that strategic thinking has become a lost art. There appears to be little reward for an executive who spends three hours thinking through various scenarios and mapping them all out. Instead, people are busy – they are always in meetings, or they are "doing" instead of thinking.

My clients understand the value of strategic thinking, and they welcome the outside perspective that myself and my

Chapter 3:
Mindset of Successful Executives

team can bring. Working with external consultants during strategy days and corporate retreats also helps create the right atmosphere for everyone to contribute and bring their best to the table. When you have someone like me to facilitate meetings and keep everything on track, it frees up everyone in your top team to contribute more fully to the discussions and formulate a strong strategy.

My role is to get the best out of your team, much like a football manager's role is to get the best out of the 11 players they have on the pitch. I want to help everyone work together towards a common goal and to ensure that everyone feels able to speak openly and debate the issues and ideas that come up in the session.

It is through these kinds of healthy debate and discussion that you can begin to future-proof your organisation. This is when you can start to lean into the uncertainty all around and focus on what needs to change to make your organisation more sustainable and long-lasting.

Uncovering the dead wood

One of my consultants always says that in any organisation, you're always going to have around ten per cent dead wood. That doesn't mean those people are useless; instead it means that they may not be able to keep up with the pace of change in a fast-growth organisation, or they may not be the right cultural fit. The executives who recognise that there is dead wood in their organisation are best placed to do something about it. That might mean moving someone into a different role or supporting them to train and grow in a new area of expertise.

Executives who have their finger on the pulse will also find it easier to identify whether someone's performance is struggling due to a temporary issue, such as going through a divorce or dealing with sickness within their family, which is causing a distraction, or whether a dip in performance is a sign that they are not the right fit for the next chapter in that organisation.

In the second scenario, it is important for a CEO to act sooner rather than later. The longer you leave such a situation to continue, the harder it will be to find options within the business that work for both parties.

A success mindset in action

Jon Rawding's first CEO role was at Euro Mechanical, and although it was a well-established business, when he joined the company he was given the opportunity to create a leadership culture and ambience that worked to help all of those within the organisation level up or, if they couldn't, to move on.

Chapter 3:

Mindset of Successful Executives

Spotlight on Jon Rawding

Role: CEO, Euro Mechanical

Tenure: February 2018–present

Biggest strengths: Willingness to listen to others; ability to motivate people and generate buy-in for change.

Achievements: Tripled the size of the company within five years.

He was very open to restructuring old divisions and to not continuing to operate as the company always had. Jon could see that the business needed some level of radical change if it was going to double in size, which was the target he had been set by the Board when he took the job.

"The previous general manager had been in the company for 33 years when I arrived, and so had hired a lot of the management team. They had a lot of experience and some of the senior guys had been there for over 40 years, so the company had a great brand and legacy. But some of the transition that needed to take place was around understanding that there was change coming.

At the start of my role at Euro Mechanical I set the scene for what was going to happen next. My first presentation was about the psychology of change management and transformation. I've been on both sides of an acquisition, so I took that experience and brought it to Euro Mechanical. I knew that people had to be aware of the emotions they were going to feel – whether that was denial, happiness, depression, anger or even acceptance.

Everyone has to understand the vision and a lot of my work at the start was around building trust, communicating and bringing the team with us. We rebranded the company and everyone

Chapter 3:
Mindset of Successful Executives

got involved so they all felt they were part of the brand."[12]

Jon worked very conscientiously alongside the Board to get the buy-in he needed from them to make the changes required within the organisation. I worked closely alongside him to create a plan to double the size of the business within five years. As it turned out, Jon was able to triple the size of the business within that timescale.

Jon embodies a growth mindset and he brings out the best in people because he spends time listening to them and coaching them. Many CEOs make the mistake of micromanaging their teams. But because they are so involved, it makes it increasingly difficult for the members of their teams to innovate or create new opportunities themselves.

In the years that I have known and worked with Jon, I have observed one of his greatest strengths to be his openness to others' ideas and his willingness to provide acknowledgement of good ideas. His biggest strengths are his ability to bring people together around the table, to motivate them and to get the buy-in that's required

---

12 *Other Side of the Business Card*, Jon Rawding (October 2021). Available at: https://www.haigbarrettpartners.com/the-other-side-of-the-business-card/episode/37593bd5/authentic-leadership-with-ceo-of-euro-mechanical-jon-rawding.

to do what needs to be done to succeed. Jon excels at being both a coach and a catalyst.

Jon also allows enough time for planning. He is happy to take people off site for a day or two to allow them to have strategic conversations, and to give people at different levels within the organisation an opportunity to ask questions about the changes being suggested. Jon hosts quarterly planning meetings, as well as weekly meetings with the executive team. He hasn't left meetings to chance. He has a plan in place to ensure that there is the space and structure to allow for robust planning.

The other way in which Jon embodies a successful executive mindset is in how he takes care of himself. He is very focused on his physical and mental health, which is important because it is easier to drive a high-performing culture when you are well-rested, are exercising regularly and are eating well. He encourages those around him to focus on their health and wellbeing.

Follow your passion

I acknowledge, and I know Jon does too, that because his current role doesn't require him to travel much for work it is much easier for him to maintain healthy routines around his diet, sleep and exercise. For CEOs like myself who travel a great deal, attend conferences and make

Chapter 3:
Mindset of Successful Executives

time to catch up with clients, it is trickier to stick to such rigorous habits.

My advice if you are in a position more like mine than Jon's is to follow your passion and look at how you can bring your lifestyle into balance where possible. That might be working from home a couple of days a week to give you the time to go for a run, or it could mean travelling a bit less for work. I know that the Covid-19 pandemic made many of us realise that we could reduce our travel and still successfully run our businesses.

The key to creating a balance that works for you is to enjoy what you do and to have a passion for your work, because without that passion your wellness will struggle.

Collaboration: a key to success

The quality of your relationships is an important factor in longevity as an individual, but this also holds true for businesses. The more long-term collaborations you can foster with partners you trust, the longer your business is likely to survive and the more successful it is likely to be.

It stands to reason that you will feel better in your work if you have partners who you can trust enough to call them when you have an issue, and vice versa, than if you are simply transacting with vendors or suppliers.

Strategic Copilot
A CEO's Guide to Changing Times

When I attended the oil and gas conference ADIPEC two years ago, there was a big focus on thinking of businesses as part of an ecosystem, where everyone wins or loses together. The conclusion that came out of these discussions was that the purely transactional approach to business would not survive the next decade. This is especially the case when you consider this alongside new industries like renewable energy that requires a great deal of investment upfront.

Ideally, businesses in sectors like energy would all invest in a plan that delivers a long-term win for everyone, within five to ten years say, and they all contribute to getting that mutually beneficial ecosystem up and running. BP took this approach with some previously unprofitable North Sea oil wells around 25 years ago. The organisation came together with its partners and encouraged everyone to work together to extract oil from the fields at a very low margin, knowing that after a couple of years they would all be able to make a considerable profit from extracting that oil.

However, it required everyone to be prepared to work for little reward in the short term, because they could see the payoff that would come in the longer term.

There are some people in this world who seem to have a talent for taking the long view. These are people who see things that others miss, and who are not afraid of

Chapter 3:
Mindset of Successful Executives

change, even if it means short-term pain on the journey to achieving their long-term goals. People who behave in this way have a strong executive mindset.

Strategic Copilot
A CEO's Guide to Changing Times

Chapter 4

The Executive Mindset in Action

I've interviewed a lot of highly successful people in the years I've been hosting my podcast, and what strikes me is that a lot of those who have great mindsets and have achieved a great deal in the business world did not perform well at school and weren't particularly academic.

On many occasions, people who have incredible executive mindsets have told me that what they learned in school, or even on an MBA programme, didn't teach them how to overcome obstacles and run through brick walls in business. This is why I'm so obsessed and fascinated by the mindset of transformation, because it isn't something you get from academic study.

Strategic Copilot
A CEO's Guide to Changing Times

After black swan events like the Covid-19 pandemic, I've noticed more and more people are interested in how those who have achieved success overcame the many obstacles in their path. All of this brings me to Terry Fisher, who is one of the most driven individuals I have ever met, as well as being someone with incredible vision and the ability to see opportunities that others have missed.

Spotlight on Terry Fisher

Role: Founder & CEO, Fisher Europa Ltd/CEO, The Craft Distilling Group

Tenure: December 2010–present/March 2024–present

Biggest strengths: His intense drive to get somewhere against all the odds.

Chapter 4:
The Executive Mindset in Action

> **Achievements:** Becoming CEO of Thomas Cook; taking just 18 months to go from idea to exit with his business Voisey, which was acquired by Snapchat in 2020.

Constant evolution

At the age of 19, Terry was made redundant from his first job and decided to take control of his own destiny. He started his own business, opening his first Travelworld store. In the following years, he grew the business to £130 million in annual turnover and increased the number of stores to 123. All of which meant he was noticed within the travel industry and his company was acquired by Airtours, which at the time of the acquisition was the UK's largest travel retailer.

But one of the stories that I feel best captures Terry's vision and ability to spot opportunities comes from his time as chairman of Huddersfield Town Football Club. The club needed a new stadium, but where does a Football League team like Huddersfield find the significant funds required for such a project? Terry realised that the location of the club's existing stadium was prime real estate that would be ideal for development into a supermarket. He also recognised that the local Rugby League club played in a stadium in a similar kind of location.

Terry went to the local council, Kirklees, and pitched his idea – why not sell both stadiums and instead build one, brand new stadium the football and rugby teams could share that was more central and more modern? With funding from the Football League, and both clubs selling their existing stadiums, they were able to build a new, 20,000-seater stadium in the centre of the town.

Attendance at the football matches increased from around 4,000 per week to 12,000 per week, because the nicer facilities at the new ground drew in a different crowd. The team also achieved promotion into what was the First Division (now the Championship) and had some good cup runs as well.[13]

Changing direction

At the age of 32, Terry decided to retire. He moved first to Marbella and then to Los Angeles, where he was very happy, although he admits that within a couple of years he had started searching for something new to give more meaning to his life. That's when he received an unexpected offer, as he told me when we spoke on the *Other Side of the Business Card* podcast.

---

13   Available at: https://www.terryfisher.com/about-me

Chapter 4:
The Executive Mindset in Action

"I was living very happily in California when I got a call to take over an ailing travel business in Preston. It was a 500-people call centre called Gold Medal Travel. Although I was happy in my life, I was looking for something significant to do and this seemed like a big job that came along at the right time.

So, I went from getting on the 405 where the signs said left to San Diego and Santa Monica, and right to Beverly Hills and La Jolla to getting on the M62 where it's left to Grimsby and Hull, and right to Rochdale and Preston!

When I took over running Gold Medal Travel, my brief was to turn it around so the owner, who was also my friend, could sell it. To cut a very long story short, I ended up doing exactly that. I knew my friend wanted to sell, and I knew in my heart that Thomas Cook was the buyer for this business. Everything I did over the next three years was with a view to selling the business to Thomas Cook.

Three years later, when it came to selling the business, Thomas Cook didn't bid for it. We had a fantastic offer on the table that the owner wanted to take, but I convinced him to give me a week to talk to Thomas Cook. Eventually, Thomas Cook did buy the business and part of the deal was that I had to sign a five-year service agreement and join their Board."[14]

What I find even more remarkable about Terry's story is that at the age of 19, when he started Travelworld, his major ambition was to become CEO of Thomas Cook. At this point, through twists of fate and his own incredible hard work and executive mindset, he had taken several steps closer to realising this dream. Within six weeks of joining the Board, Terry became CEO and realised his lifelong ambition.

Creating a culture of openness

In my career I have been lucky to meet and work with many people who embody an executive mindset, and one of those is Tony Meggs, former Chair of Crossrail, who joined me on the *Between the Lines with Haig* podcast.

One of the things I found fascinating about him was his reaction to being asked to take over as Chair of Crossrail at a time when the project was receiving a great deal of negative press for being over budget and not delivering as expected.

---

[14] *Other Side of the Business Card*, Terry Fisher (September 2021). Available at: https://www.haigbarrettpartners.com/the-other-side-of-the-business-card/episode/2492ee9f/running-2-x-billion-dollar-businesses-with-entrepreneur-terry-fisher.

Chapter 4:
The Executive Mindset in Action

Before stepping into the Crossrail hot seat, Tony was part of the Infrastructure and Projects Authority where he would often comment on how Crossrail could be better run. When he was given the opportunity to take the lead on the project, his executive mindset kicked in and his reaction wasn't, "you must be kidding", but in fact was: "I'd better put my money where my mouth is and see what I can do".

Spotlight on Tony Meggs

Role: Chair, Crossrail Ltd

Tenure: January 2019–October 2020

Biggest strengths: His ability to bring people to the table and create alignment.

Achievements: Turning around the Crossrail project.

Strategic Copilot
A CEO's Guide to Changing Times

When Tony stepped into the top Crossrail job, the project was in disarray. Despite being well run for a long time, it had hit challenges that had completely derailed it. Things had gone spectacularly wrong for complicated reasons, as Tony explained to me when we spoke.

> "In some ways, the thing that had created the success of the original team also led to its failure. The team lost track and didn't really understand what was left to be done. We had to come along and reprogramme the whole thing. That meant doing three things.
>
> One was to build a new team. The second was to build a new plan, which was actually harder than we thought. And the third was to build confidence, because trust and confidence was completely eroded with the stakeholders, the sponsors, the people paying the bills and the public. Rebuilding trust was a huge amount of my work."[15]

Tony used a lot of the leadership and development techniques that I recommend to my clients for creating alignment and building trust, which are based on the work of Werner Erhard. One of the big challenges Tony faced

---

15 *Between the Lines with Haig*, Tony Meggs (March 2021). Available at: https://www.haigbarrettpartners.com/between-the-lines-with-haig/episode/291cc63c/episode-7-tony-meggs-fast-tracks-the-future.

Chapter 4:
The Executive Mindset in Action

initially was getting everyone to be honest about the real timelines and costs for the remainder of the project.

Until this point, everyone had been agreeing to proposed timelines and costs, even if they didn't feel they were realistic, because they feared getting into trouble. What Tony did incredibly well was to bring everyone together and facilitate open discussions that allowed him and the rest of the team to rebuild plans, get everyone to commit to realistic project timescales and budgets, and ultimately bring the whole project back on track.

Simplifying the complex

What I hadn't fully appreciated before I spoke to Tony was the complexity of the Crossrail project. Take Paddington Station as an example – there are eight floors underground and something in the order of 500 individual rooms, each of which contains complicated electrical equipment. The platforms themselves are twice the length of a normal tube platform, and about four times the width to accommodate full-sized trains.

In total, there are 42 Crossrail stations in London, of which ten are major new stations – like Paddington. Tony explained that the average underground station in London has around 200 data collection points, whereas each Crossrail station has 2,200, making it amazingly sophisticated. This means someone in Romford is able to see when a light bulb goes out in Paddington.

Tony is rightly proud of being part of the project to create what he describes as "a truly digital railway that is a whole magnitude more sophisticated than what's come before".

Building foundations for success, even in failure

When I met Andrew Richardson, Managing Director of Home House, I quickly realised that we were quite similar in how we approach life and handle setbacks. Neither of us dwell on failure, instead we use those experiences to propel us into something better.

Chapter 4:

The Executive Mindset in Action

Spotlight on Andrew Richardson

Role: Managing Director, Home House

Tenure: May 2008–present

Biggest strengths: His openness to what might come next and confidence in his abilities.

Achievements: Transforming the Home House business by building on the original creator's desire to create a "Palace of Pleasure".

One of the things I enjoyed about my conversation with Andrew was how open he was about his early years. Like many of us, as a teenager he had no idea what he wanted to do with his life. He found a job as a pot washer in a local hotel. His work ethic shone through, and it wasn't long before the chefs were giving him bits of prep work to do in the kitchen.

This set him on a path to a highly successful career in hospitality, where he worked his way up to head chef in some very impressive establishments all over the world. Eventually, Andrew moved back to the UK and bought his own gastropub. However, this dream wasn't meant to be as the pub flooded and he was forced to sell and seek employment.

He went to work for a hotel management company, helping to turn around several country house hotels in the UK. It was during this period that he was spotted by Home House and asked to join the organisation. Since joining the company in 2008, Andrew has overseen its expansion and came up with the idea of creating a secondary brand, Home Grown, designed to build a community specifically to support entrepreneurs on their growth journeys.

This is an important point of differentiation from the Home House brand, which is very focused on the social aspect of members' clubs, whereas Home Grown is unashamedly about business. Its members are experienced entrepreneurs, high-growth entrepreneurs, sophisticated investors and trusted advisers. Everything about it, from the rooms and meeting rooms in each of

Chapter 4:
The Executive Mindset in Action

its clubs, to the events the organisation facilitates, is designed to support entrepreneurs.

Open and honest

What struck me about Andrew's journey is that he never planned a particular career trajectory, but things came to him. Like many of the business leaders featured in this book, he was open to seeing things beyond his immediate field of vision. This meant that he could spot opportunities that arose, rather than being so focused on a specific plan that he was blind to anything that didn't fit in with that roadmap.

What Andrew has done incredibly well is taken all of his previous experiences, good and bad, and used them to build a foundation for future success. One of his greatest strengths throughout his career is his ability to build strong relationships and how much he cares for the people who work for him.

During our conversation on the Other Side of the Business Card podcast, he told me how he dealt with the Brexit vote in 2016, given that he had many European members of staff on his team.

> "When the Brexit vote went in a way that I certainly hadn't expected it to, I felt really bad

for our European members of staff because the human side of it was awful for them. Here they were, working in a historic members' club in London and all of a sudden the majority of the population had said 'we don't want you here'.

I spent a good few days speaking to as many of them as possible in person, reassuring them honestly that this was not what I or the business wanted or what we expected. I didn't want them to feel that they weren't valued."[16]

To me, this demonstrates what an amazing person he is to work for, as well as the value of caring for your team in both good and bad times.

All of the business leaders I've highlighted in this part of the book are great examples of the executive mindset at work, and show how embracing this mindset can lead to success. A common thread among all of them is openness and a willingness to transform, both personally and professionally, to support the businesses they work with to survive and thrive in an ever-changing world.

---

16 *Other Side of the Business Card*, Andrew Richardson (February 2021). Available at: https://www.haigbarrettpartners.com/the-other-side-of-the-business-card/episode/1ed695b6/home-houses-md-andrew-richardson.

Chapter 4:
The Executive Mindset in Action

To access additional resources around the theme of building an executive team, scan the following QR code:

Strategic Copilot
A CEO's Guide to Changing Times

Transformation: Preparing and Staying on Track

Once you have found the right people to be part of your executive team, or have helped your existing executive team to shift their mindset towards one focused on growth and transformation, you can start to explore transformation within the wider business.

There are several fundamental concepts required as you prepare for transformation. The first, which we'll discuss in Chapter 5, is a solid grasp of your current position. Without knowing what your base is, you cannot hope to build on it. With this understanding, you can develop a step-out growth strategy that will accelerate your transformation and business performance.

To enact that strategy effectively, you need to have the right leadership team in place. You also need to have a clear strategy for communicating the strategic change to the wider organisation. Creating buy-in for the long-term vision is essential to give you the confidence to flatten your organisational hierarchy and provide those working for you with greater autonomy.

Chapter 5

Understanding and Defending Your Base

Before you can build a step-out growth strategy to facilitate transformation, you need to understand your starting point – your base. There are three components to understanding your base:

1. Having the right team in place.

2. Having a structured toolkit that drives strategy, products and market.

3. Having a governing structure and processes in place.

Strategic Copilot
A CEO's Guide to Changing Times

The challenge for many leaders is that they are very driven, which makes it much more exciting to look at a shiny new object rather than focusing on the existing object that is in front of them. The risk of chasing the shiny new object all the time is that you lose the support of the people who are going to look after your base and defend it, which can ultimately have a detrimental effect on your business.

When you are exploring new avenues for growth and transformation you therefore need to begin by having an understanding of your foundations. You need to make the people on your team who will be running – or defending – your core business feel just as valued as those who will be working on the new venture.

As a CEO, you always need to look after that core business. If you notice that revenues are going down, your priority should be to bring more cash into the core business, rather than to shelve innovation projects.

Finally, when you can effectively defend your base, you will be much better placed to identify genuine opportunities for growth for your business. I think it's fair to say that many people want to be part of a lot of different spaces, but that isn't always practical or advisable if you don't have the knowledge or capabilities to support that.

Chapter 5:
Understanding and Defending Your Base

When you have a good understanding of your core business, you will be able to make a decision about which markets to move into based on the capabilities you already have, which markets you already have a solid understanding of and which customers you already own or know will support you. A growth strategy for an existing business should be an extension of what you already do and know, rather than a completely new startup in an unknown field. By framing your growth strategy in these terms, you can take care of your business and defend it.

Having the right leadership team in place

Before you create a step-out growth strategy, you need to understand what you've got. There's no better way to see what you have than by having a leadership team who knows what is going on in every area of the business. In my experience, many CEOs and executives do not have their fingers on the pulse of every part of their business.

Your team, or external consultants if you don't have the right top team in place already, should be able to help you understand which areas of your business are in the growth stage, which are maintaining the status quo and which are in the decline stage. The reason having the right team is important is that they will be able to work with you to build a strategy that defends your core business. Based on their knowledge, you can then build out the next phase of your business without undermining what you have already created.

One of the biggest mistakes I see leaders making is not putting enough energy into understanding and defending their core business. When it comes to the people on your team, you also have to ask whether you have the right types of people for the stage that your business is in. For example, if you have a mature business, you will want someone to head it up who has a track record of maintaining organisations, rather than someone who is a bit more of a wild explorer. This will give you the space and confidence to explore growth strategies, knowing that you have someone who's watching your back.

In my 25-plus years of consulting, one of the biggest challenges I've noticed, particularly for new CEOs coming into an organisation, is that they inherit a team, while at the same time putting together a new plan for the business or a division. In other words, there is a lot going on.

In such a situation, it's understandable that you might focus on the plan, rather than taking a deep dive into your team. But it's essential that you make time to understand how good your inherited team is and whether they are a good fit for what you want to do to move the company forward.

Chapter 5:
Understanding and Defending Your Base

Having external support, such as an experienced consultant, can be incredibly helpful for assessing the leadership team and working out who is good at defending the core business and who will be best able to support the step-out growth you are aiming for. I'll talk in much greater detail about how to develop your leadership team and ensure they are ready for change in Chapter 7.

Tips for creating alignment in your team

It is best to find out how aligned people are with your vision one-on-one, rather than in a boardroom meeting that can easily descend into an argument. Take the time to speak to each of your executives about their thoughts on the direction and strategy of the business.

You have to play a political game here – what might you need to do to get someone on board? Is there anything you can offer them to ensure their support in front of the Board?

This means that when you all come back together, you can be confident that everyone in your top team aligns around the strategy and vision for the business.

Having a structured toolkit that drives strategy, products and market

There are numerous tools you can use for this purpose, but the one I use most frequently is the strategy diamond approach. This brings together your mission, objectives and strategic analysis to create a strategy which then determines the supporting organisational arrangements you need in place – such as structure, process, people, policies and so on.[17]

I always start by taking my clients through the three Cs: the customer, the competition and the company itself. Many organisations already have the data they need through tools they already use, such as SWOT (strengths, weaknesses, opportunities, threats) analysis, and information they've gathered on their different customer segments. Once we have all of this information, we look at competitors.

Finally, we focus on the environment in which the business operates. We tend to keep our focus on the short term, so one to three years. When I first started consulting over 20 years ago, we would also look at the long-term environment over a ten-year timeline, but things change

---

17   Hambrick, D.C. and Fredrickson, J.W. (2005) "Are you sure you have a strategy?," *Academy of Management Perspectives*, 19(4), pp. 51–62. Available at: https://doi.org/10.5465/ame.2005.19417907.

Chapter 5:
Understanding and Defending Your Base

so quickly nowadays that we rarely look beyond three years ahead. All of this feeds into the strategy.

The strategy is a diamond comprising four areas: arenas, vehicles, differentiators and staging. The arenas part of this diamond is all about understanding where you play. How can you defend your base? And also where you want to play – in other words, what areas you want to move into through your step-out growth strategy.

Next we look at vehicles, which can be anything that will help you deliver success. This could be technology, it could be intellectual property (IP) or it could even be the quality your organisation delivers.

When I'm working with executives who are struggling to articulate their core capabilities and the vehicles that will drive the strategy, I ask them to imagine they are being featured on the front cover of *Forbes* magazine three years from now, and that they're being interviewed about their success. The vehicles for this strategy will be the two or three things you would say underpinned that success. In other words, the vehicles are the two or three elements where you were a cut above the rest.

Then we move on to the differentiators, which are the advantages of the strategy you've created. How will you win in this space? Will it be due to your image, price, customisation, product reliability, quality or something else?

Finally, we have staging, which is basically the timing. You look at the near term – one to six months – and the longer term, one to three years, and you work out what you want to deliver when within that timescale. Once you have all four of these elements in place, you will have a solid strategy with which to move forward.

We then take this strategy and plot it on what we call the implementation star, which has five points. Strategy sits at the top, with the other four points covering:

- The structure of the company and how it works, as well as the number of offices, warehouses and other facilities.
- The people within the business.
- Information systems, which covers everything from the CRM (customer relationship management) and ERP (enterprise resource planning) to regular meetings with the CEO and any quarterly offsites.
- Rewards – based on the projected success, what are the rewards?

Finally, in the centre of the star are what we call symbols. These are activities that the business plans to undertake that need to align with the broader strategy. For example, let's say you've recently taken over a division and want to streamline the core business initially, which means laying people off. In that instance, you wouldn't want

Chapter 5:
Understanding and Defending Your Base

to spend money on flashy events because that doesn't align with people potentially losing their jobs.

By contrast, if you're a business in Silicon Valley that's trying to attract the best people and aiming to double in size, you might want to host fancy parties at the Four Seasons, for instance, to project the right image.

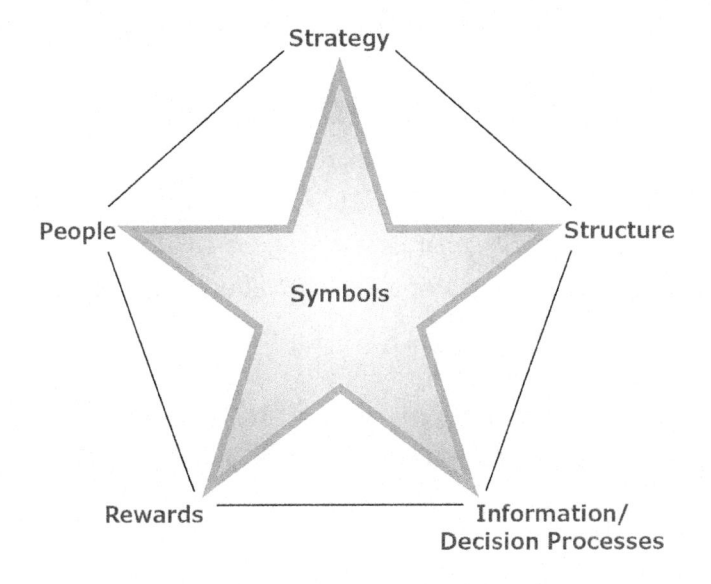

```
              Strategy
               /\
              /  \
             /    \
   People ──┤ Symbols ├── Structure
             \    /
              \  /
               \/
        Rewards    Information/
                   Decision Processes
```

It's important that you work through this process in the order I've set out here, because the information you gather at each stage builds the foundations for the next one.

In my experience, many companies have the data I've just mentioned already, but what they lack is the ability to bring it together as much as they need to in order to really accelerate their growth. The key to getting the most from this process is fully understanding your base and working out how you can grow from there. The value of a consultant like myself is that me and my team can bring data together and interrogate it in a different way.

We know the right questions to ask to help you uncover your truly unique competitive advantage. Often this isn't what you might be familiar with from reading around the business world. Where you make the biggest gains is often on the boundaries and by digging out the observations and knowledge that haven't yet been made publicly available. This is what can actually be what gives you a head start when you're trying to outmanoeuvre your competitors.

As a large enterprise, it is often much better to empower your employees within different divisions to make decisions. In doing so, you go from being one large enterprise to being thousands of microenterprises, each of which has complete power to run itself. The idea is to achieve zero distance to customer – in other words, to ensure that each of your teams can anticipate what its customers want, perhaps even before they know that for themselves.

This is the kind of autonomy William talked about earlier in the book. In this kind of organisation, teams

Chapter 5:
Understanding and Defending Your Base

are empowered to make decisions on the ground and can therefore adapt and react quickly to changing circumstances. There is no need to wait for higher-level management signoff, provided the decisions align with the company's overall direction of travel.

Case study: Haier

Chinese appliance company Haier is a great example of a large enterprise that has embraced the concept of empowering its employees to allow them to find those opportunities on the boundaries, and act on them quickly.

During the Covid-19 pandemic, one of Haier's employees was attending his vaccination appointment when he noticed a problem. The doors on some of the refrigerators holding the Covid-19 vaccines weren't automatically closing once a vaccine had been removed. This meant the temperature within the fridge would fluctuate and could potentially damage the vaccines.

After noticing this issue, he went back to work and was given the budget to run a small project to design fridges specifically for holding vaccinations. The pilot was a huge success and the product was launched to the wider market. During the Covid-19 pandemic, this

> became a highly profitable division for Haier, making the company millions.
>
> The reason I highlight this example is because, had no one at Haier acted until there were news reports of vaccines being rendered ineffective because of fridge doors being left open, then the company would have been in a race with its competitors to design a vaccine refrigerator. But because one employee saw a need for this product and was empowered to act, the company was able to develop something and release it to market before its competitors even knew it was a problem that needed to be solved.

Having a governing structure and processes in place

I believe that one of the most important things a CEO does is manage their top team, which is an essential aspect of the governing structure. There needs to be a process for how the leadership team knows when to escalate issues to the CEO.

The CEO has a judicial responsibility to report to the Board and to manage the company's investments and finance. Therefore, the CEO needs the right communication

Chapter 5:
Understanding and Defending Your Base

paths to their executives and to quality control in the organisation to support them in this responsibility.

Part of that structure involves setting decision rights – who has the right to make decisions about what. These decision rights cascade down, so the CEO will set out decision rights with their executives, who will then set out decision rights with their teams and so on throughout the organisation. Often these decision rights will relate to the level of spending an individual can sign off on.

In many larger organisations, while the CEO will have overall rights in terms of the company's banking and financials, there will often need to be someone who is authorised to co-sign large transactions and even to process payroll each month. This means there also needs to be a backup process should the CEO or relevant co-signer not be available for any reason.

It's important to note that these kinds of governance structures get built out over time and as a business grows you need different levels of controls. As your business gets bigger, you will almost certainly need a compliance officer to ensure you are adhering to all the relevant regulations within your industry.

Many mid-sized organisations that are in high-growth mode need support to ensure the right structures and processes are in place. Often it's necessary to bring in an external consultant to conduct a risk analysis. This consultant can ensure, firstly, that all the right compliance structures are in place, and secondly help you as the CEO find the right people to take ownership of certain areas.

All of these processes need to be written down or turned into workflows. Although this can feel like a lot of effort, I can honestly say that in my 25 years of consulting I have never seen a workflow that we've mapped out not pay dividends. These workflows improve your understanding of your business and support you with training your team.

Most situations that you're likely to encounter will need to have a workflow around them, particularly on the operational side of the business. These workflows should include escalation procedures, which feed into your company governance. I'm a firm believer in having a project management office, because although this might seem like an expense, it will save you a great deal by keeping projects on track.

Toyota has been a client of mine for 20 years and one of the biggest gifts they have given me is the insight into their well-documented A3 strategy execution visuals. Workflows are key and, even if we're not producing detailed workflows for a client, we will always produce a workflow at a macro level, usually in the form of an A3 workflow document. In 2009, the *MIT Sloan Management Review* wrote an article taking a deep dive into how Toyota

Chapter 5:
Understanding and Defending Your Base

built these A3 documents, what they achieve and how effective they are.[18]

When I was just starting out in consulting 25 years ago, companies would measure efficiency by analysing manufacturing processes as they had clear metrics for productivity. These companies would therefore put less emphasis on improving the management of other areas of business development, which had a lower improvement in efficiency than manufacturing as a result.

I've certainly seen companies over the years lose a considerable amount of money simply because they didn't have a project management office and strong workflows in place. As a hypothetical example, let's imagine that when the request for proposal (RFP) stage was carried out, the business rejected a proposal at $500,000 and went for the cheaper option at $350,000. However, because of the lack of process around the $350,000 offer, the eventual spend on the project was $1 million.

Now imagine that you're heading up a large company and all of your projects are running over by similar margins. What would it mean for your business if you could reduce those costs by up to 70 per cent? This is what you can

---

18   Shook, J. (2009) "Toyota's secret: the A3 report." *MIT Sloan Management Review*. Available at: https://sloanreview.mit.edu/article/toyotas-secret-the-a3-report/.

achieve when you have the right project managers in place and provide the right level of project management training to your staff.

We've worked with clients where we have been able to reduce their bid prices by up to 70 per cent simply by putting project management workflows and structures in place. In some cases, my team even rewrote RFPs to ensure there was complete clarity about what the business wanted and what the price should be.

In one instance, the company hired ten project managers and because of the work we did with them to introduce workflows and better project management, those ten project managers were essentially cost neutral for the business because of the level of savings they generated.

Advice to understand and defend your base

1. Understand alignment across your whole business – to what extent is your Board aligned with your strategy? What about your top team? Score their alignment out of ten, and if it's lower than ten, spend some time working out what you need to do to be ten/ten aligned.

2. Get clear on your strategy and share that with your teams. Empower them to make decisions and

Chapter 5:
Understanding and Defending Your Base

support them to develop ideas that could drive the company towards its goals.

3. Audit your governance structure and decision rights. Create a mindmap of all the governance procedures in your company and make sure that there are no gaps and that everyone is aligned around these procedures.

Strategic Copilot
A CEO's Guide to Changing Times

Chapter 6:
Your Step-Out Growth Strategy

Your Step-Out Growth Strategy

Before considering step-out growth, one of the first things I recommend doing is what we've discussed in the previous chapter – making sure that you have a clear understanding of your core business and its growth rates. For many companies, focusing on growing their core business is sufficient. If this is where you are, then take the time to focus on understanding and defending your base.

Step-out growth is different. This is when you either develop new products for your existing customers, take existing products to new geographical markets or decide to develop something completely different. This third option is the hardest to get right, because you're creating a new product that doesn't appeal to either your current customer base or your current market.

You can achieve step-out growth organically, that's to say solely through what you produce and do as a business. Or you can achieve it through mergers and acquisitions (M&A), which may also involve building out new sets of companies into new industries.

One of the most important things to do in the early days of your step-out growth phase is to ensure you have the right people to both defend your core business and grow into new areas. In fact, I'd say that around 50 per cent of the time you spend developing your step-out growth strategy will be dedicated to finding the right people.

This might involve hiring in from the outside or even seeking new business partners. In some cases you may decide to develop partnerships or distribution networks. I talk in more detail about finding the right people for your leadership team specifically, and how to manage change with them, in the next chapter.

Taking a leap of faith

Often, a step-out growth strategy requires a leap of faith – or what Jim Collins called a "big, hairy, audacious

Chapter 6:
Your Step-Out Growth Strategy

goal" in his book *Good to Great*.[19] One company that has done this incredibly well is Toyota.

I've worked with them as a consultant for over 20 years, and I feel very privileged to have been shown some of the documents about the development of their first hybrid vehicle – the Prius. The documents I was shown revealed that Toyota started developing the Prius about ten years before they launched it. The fact that they had seen the potential for the electrification of vehicles so far in advance is amazing.

Initially, the Prius was launched into the US market, where Toyota made a loss of around $6,000 per car sold. But they were committed and the company was happy to pay the subsidy on those vehicles to be known as the first automaker to step into the hybrid world. Of course, within just a few years of its launch, the Prius became one of the world's topselling cars.

But they had to do a lot of work to both develop the technology and then sell it to drivers. All the staff in the 1,200 or so of the Toyota dealerships in the USA needed to be trained not only in how to sell a car that was so different to every other model on the market, but also in how to service a vehicle that had hybrid-battery

---

19 Collins, J.C. (2001) Good to Great: *Why Some Companies Make the Leap – and Others Don't*. Random House.

technology. Everything was new, but this is an excellent example of step-out growth.

I spoke to Executive Vice-President of Toyota, Jack Hollis, on the *Other Side of the Business Card*, and he offered some fascinating insights into the courage it took to commit to the Prius as a concept.

Spotlight on Jack Hollis

Role: EVP and Chief Operating Officer, Toyota North America

Tenure: April 2024–present; although has held various positions within Toyota since 2007.

Biggest strengths: His leadership and transformation mindset, and the care he shows for everyone he meets.

Chapter 6:
Your Step-Out Growth Strategy

> **Achievements:** Named as one of the 50 most innovative CMOs by *Business Insider* in 2017; twice named *Automotive News* All-Star.

Jack told me that when Toyota launched the Prius in the USA and the UK, many within the automotive industry mocked the company.

> "The leaders of most other companies in the industry mocked us, saying: 'You can't change the gas engine.' ... We were the first ones in EVs (electric vehicles) over 20 years ago with our Rav4, and they mocked us then. Then they mocked the Prius hybrid and our plug-in hybrid. Then we bring out the fuel cell and they're mocking us again. But I laugh because Toyota has always been at the leading edge of what we believe our customers want. We're simply trying to provide that as safely and as soon as possible." [20]

Toyota has continued to innovate since I had that conversation with Jack and it remains an excellent

---

20 *Other Side of the Business Card*, Jack Hollis (September 2021). Available at: https://www.haigbarrettpartners.com/the-other-side-of-the-business-card/episode/2899c54e/the-future-of-mobility-with-toyotas-senior-vice-president-of-automotive-operations-jack-hollis.

example of what's possible when a company is bold enough to not only explore step-out growth options, but to commit to them.

There are similar stories throughout the world of business – just think back to the reception the Apple iPad received when it was launched. Many people laughed at the name, and at the concept in general, but it was an important part of the company's core strategy shift towards mobility in computing. It was a similar story when Apple launched the iPod. Within a few short years this device had annihilated the Sony Walkman, which had previously dominated the portable music market.

What's interesting is that Apple wasn't the first company to launch an MP3 player, but what differentiated Apple's offering was iTunes. By sticking to its growth strategy and understanding that it wasn't only about the player itself, but also about how easy it was for users to load music on to the player, the company outpaced all its competitors within months of launching.

The value of an outside view

In my experience, the biggest problem companies have when trying to identify opportunities for step-out growth is that they spend too much time talking to people who already know what they know. Even if representatives

Chapter 6:
Your Step-Out Growth Strategy

from the organisation go to big conferences or shows, they often spend most of their time talking to the distributors and contacts they already know.

One of the best pieces of advice I can give you, therefore, is to spend just ten per cent of your time talking to people that you wouldn't normally consider or perhaps even want to talk to, just to get a different perspective.

If you can afford it, bringing in an outside consultant can help you to bulletproof your strategies. You might find someone like me annoying, because I ask a lot of questions. I won't be satisfied to take the answer your distributor gave you at face value. I'll force you to check your information. But this will help you get a much better handle on your strategy and spot any holes before they become so big they sink the business.

The other area where a consultant such as myself can help is with strategic foresight, which I'll cover in much greater depth later in the book. But as a starting point, you need a strategy to allow people within your company to constantly scan the environment you're in and look out for strong or weak signals that will either support your strategy or act as a leading indicator that you may need to change direction.

What has become evident since 2020 is that you can't rely entirely on one core strategy. You need to not only have a plan A, but also plans B, C, D and E. One of the tools we use with our clients is the Five-Futures strategy, where you map out your core strategy, and then two higher-growth strategies above it, and two lower-growth strategies below it. The advantage of this approach is that it allows you to pivot much more rapidly if the landscape changes for better or for worse.

Let's consider a business operating in the oil and gas industry as an example. Four years ago, it may not have been important for them to monitor the price of steel more than quarterly. However, as I write this, due to various wars happening around the world that have disrupted production and shipping routes, they will likely need to be monitoring it week by week.

What I would describe as a "weak signal" that this was on the cards occurred in mid-2021. I was travelling to the UAE and I asked a few people there whether they thought Russia would invade Ukraine. The people I spoke to at that time felt there was a chance Russia could invade. To me that was a weak signal that something might happen that could impact various elements of any business, but particularly those companies doing business with people or organisations in Russia.

When you spot this kind of weak signal, it's important to start to map out how that could affect your business. As it turned out, just a few months later Russia invaded

Chapter 6:
Your Step-Out Growth Strategy

Ukraine. Anyone else who had seen that as a possibility around the same time that I did would therefore have had at least three months to come up with contingency plans for that eventuality.

A "strong signal", meanwhile, was when Russian ships blockaded the Black Sea, preventing Ukrainian vessels from transporting grain and other products out of the country. This indicated that shipping of certain products and from certain locations would take longer and cost considerably more in the coming months.

As the CEO, you need to be looking for both strong and weak signals. When you spot them, you need to communicate those signals to your operations team so that they can find solutions. In the world in which we now live, you need to be having such conversations at least once a quarter with your team, because situations can, and do, change rapidly.

Of course, not all scenario planning is based around conflict like this. Another example of how to plan for different scenarios could be thinking about what would happen if your competitors successfully pinched some of your key staff. In this instance, one of the scenarios you planned for would be lower performance if you were unable to retain your top executive talent.

Another example could be recognising the value of your top salesperson. Your plan B might revolve around the idea that if you don't pay that person enough, they could leave. If they left, how quickly could you replace them? If the hiring process will take longer than six months then that one salesperson's departure could affect your business for a full year.

When you work with an external consultant, it is much easier to have open conversations that consider all manner of possibilities. As a consultant, it's not necessarily that I know more about an industry or company than the executives, but what I do know is how to lead a conversation and explore a range of possibilities in great enough detail that it is useful.

We use a specific futures analysis tool that was developed by one of my consultants, which looks at your most probable future as a business, as well as the antithesis of that future. In doing so, you can identify which tasks and actions are the same in either future. You can also see which ones may need to change depending on what happens in the environment in which you operate.

In most cases, 90 per cent of tasks remain the same and there are just 10 per cent that would vary between the two scenarios. In this situation, you would work towards your most probable future, while investing resources to help you counter the antithesis of that future. This means

Chapter 6:
Your Step-Out Growth Strategy

even if the unlikely antithesis comes to pass, you are ready to counter its effects on your business.

Creating your Five-Futures

The following are some questions you can work through to help you create your Five-Futures strategy.

What is your core strategy?

- What is the central approach your business currently relies on for growth and stability?
- What are the foundational elements, and how do they address your market's needs?

What would a high-growth future look like?

- What are two scenarios where growth accelerates beyond your current expectations?
- What external or internal factors (such as technological breakthroughs, market expansion or competitive shifts) could drive this growth?
- How would your business capitalise on these opportunities?

What would a low-growth future look like?

Imagine two scenarios where growth slows or declines.

- What factors (such as market contraction, geopolitical events or resource scarcity) might cause this?
- How would your business adapt to minimise any impact?

How will you identify and act on weak and strong signals?

Develop a process for monitoring your industry and the global landscape.

- What weak signals might indicate a need for adjustment?
- What strong signals would confirm the need for change?
- How will you incorporate these into your planning?

What elements of your strategy are consistent across all futures?

Examine your workflows, resources and operational tasks to identify the 90 per cent that remains stable regardless of the scenario.

- How can you optimise these elements to ensure resilience, while allocating resources to prepare for the ten per cent that might vary?

Chapter 6:
Your Step-Out Growth Strategy

Whatever these different futures look like, you need a team who can lead you through any of them. Who you have on your leadership team is a crucial factor that can determine your business' success or failure.

Strategic Copilot
A CEO's Guide to Changing Times

Chapter 7

Leadership Team

As I explained in Chapter 5, having the right team in place is essential if you are aiming for high growth within your organisation. Often one of the biggest challenges is managing change and bringing everyone with you. Before you roll out any new strategy, your top team needs to be aligned around it so that you present a united front to everyone else in the business.

Managing change and expectations

Most of the clients I am lucky enough to work with have big growth plans. As a result, I regularly advise about how to communicate change and how to get buy-in for that change.

As a general rule of thumb, one-third of an organisation won't want to change, one-third will want to change and one-third will be somewhere in the middle. Therefore, you're always going to have to deal with around one-third of people in your organisation who aren't directly opposed to change, but who don't want things to change too fast. In this case, you can typically work with about half of them.

As a leader, the key is to use techniques to make the journey so exciting for them that, even if they don't want to change, they will enjoy the journey with you. To bring as many people with you as possible, you have to do a lot of work before you begin the change process.

In some of the companies I've worked with, myself and my team will spend time getting to know what drives the people within it who are not looking for change. For example, someone who is two years from retirement might want to maintain the status quo and not shake things up too much. Meanwhile, someone else in the same position might be excited by the prospect of supporting a new business division in getting off the ground and see that as their way of leaving a legacy.

I would estimate that around one-third of the value I bring as a consultant in any project is through dealing with people. Often this means elegantly getting the wrong people out. I don't necessarily mean that they're fired,

Chapter 7:
Leadership Team

but that they might move to a division where they'll be a better fit and hopefully enjoy their work more as a result.

If you are building a high-growth organisation, my advice is to hire a HR manager at an executive level. Too many times I've seen a CEO get bogged down by people management. They have good intentions for wanting to be involved in all of the hiring decisions, however, they don't fully understand the amount of time and work it takes to manage people who don't want to embrace change. When up to one-third of your workforce falls into this category, there is a lot to deal with. If you don't manage transitions properly, especially if you are letting people go, it can get messy very quickly.

This is why I believe having someone with senior HR experience is important. Similarly, if your business is growing rapidly, you will also be hiring quickly. Again, having someone with a great deal of experience in a HR role will serve you well and help ensure you can defend your base by bringing in the right people, rather than hiring the wrong people.

I often encounter business leaders who are reluctant to hire people into positions for their expected growth. Let's say they have the ambition to grow the business by 30 per cent in two years, but they don't want to hire people for that 30 per cent growth until they've achieved it. However, by not hiring early, they hold back their organisation's growth potential and reduce their chances of hitting the target.

If we're being realistic, the hiring process takes a minimum of three months and often closer to a year, especially for executive-level positions. So, if you're confident you can hit that growth target, you need to start building out certain parts of that team before you achieve the growth you're aiming for. The way I see it, when you look at augmenting your HR and legal teams, the expense is minimal in percentage terms compared to the investment you're making to grow the business.

The good news is that, in my experience, leaders who are charismatic and forward-looking often find it relatively quick to find the right people. Their growth plans naturally attract the right people into the organisation, which accelerates the hiring process.

This is why I would also advise not only developing a strong growth strategy, but vocalising it, whether that's on LinkedIn, another social media platform or via a press release. In doing so, you will often find you attract people who are not only of a high calibre, but who also want to work for you because they believe in the strategy you've set out.

Chapter 7:
Leadership Team

Psychometric tools for team management

Myself and my team find psychometric testing tools particularly useful for helping work out who fits where in organisations, and who is a good fit overall for a team. Although we use a plethora of tools, one of the ones I find most effective is the Team Management Survey (TMS) designed by Margerison-McCann. I've used this both with my own team and many of the companies I've worked with over the last 25 years.

The reason I like it is because it is similar to Myers-Briggs, which most people have heard of. However, it presents the results in a very simple way by plotting each team member on to a circle where it's clear to see what their strengths are, and therefore how each person contributes and complements the other members of an executive team.

Strategic Copilot
A CEO's Guide to Changing Times

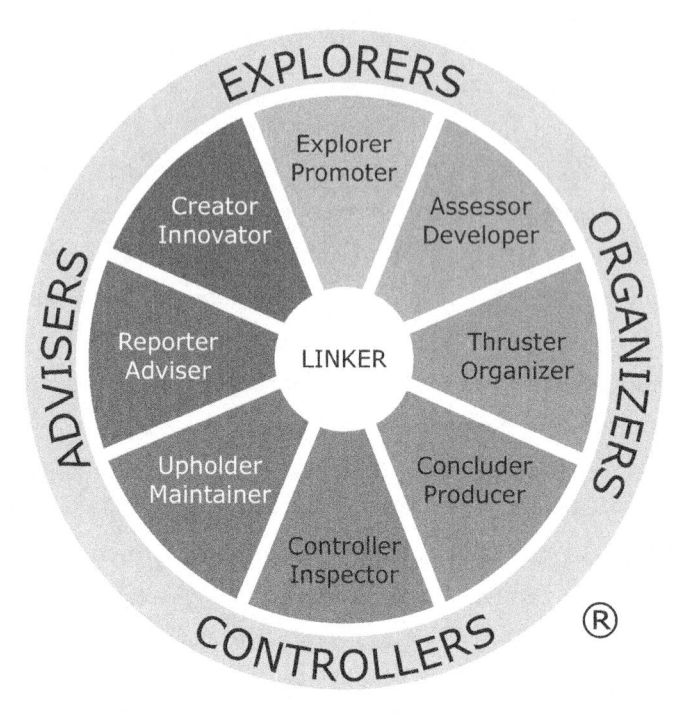

EXPLORERS
- Explorer Promoter
- Creator Innovator
- Assessor Developer

ORGANIZERS
- Thruster Organizer
- Concluder Producer

CONTROLLERS
- Controller Inspector
- Upholder Maintainer

ADVISERS
- Reporter Adviser

LINKER ®

Credit: Team Management Survey (TMS), https://www.teammanagementsystems.com/our-products/team-management-profile-tmp/

On some occasions, I've run this exercise with Boards and every person in an executive team of eight has come out exactly the same. You might think that sounds great, because you'll all share the same views. However, this is not the case. The difficulty is, if all of your Board wants to behave in the same way, you won't achieve anything meaningful.

Chapter 7:
Leadership Team

For example, let's say every member of your Board comes in as an explorer/promoter. This puts them at the top of a vertical axis with extroverts at the top and introverts at the bottom. They'll all want to seek out new opportunities, but there will be no one to record what's been done, by whom and what progress has been made.

You need to hire a balanced team to ensure that every aspect of the business receives the attention it needs, and that every person in your leadership team complements the others.

Another tool that we use, Insights®, explores what you might describe as a more horizontal analysis. This is colour-based and separates people's traits out by whether they fall into red, yellow, green or blue. As an overview, these are described as follows:

- Red: driver. These people tend to be bold, quick to act and focus on results.
- Yellow: expressive. Yellows are very social, enjoy talking and are typically quite extrovert.
- Green: amiable. People in this camp are all about the team and focus strongly on relationships.
- Blue: analytical. Blues are deep thinkers and happy to work alone at their desk for days at a time.

There is no right and wrong when it comes to what balance of these traits each team needs. Ideally, however, you want a blend of all of them. Therefore, by carrying out these kinds of exercises we can very quickly see what's missing. In some cases, it isn't that anything is missing as such. In such instances, this exercise allows us to bring the team together and help them see how they fit together.

One of the most important additional benefits of these exercises is that it helps teams understand one another's communication styles. Sometimes my team will bring in actors who role-play different personality types, so that everyone can practise interacting with others who are not the same "colour" as them. This can have a profound positive impact.

For example, we ran this kind of session with a large pharmaceutical company team recently, which had a very strong "red" leader. Throughout the course of just half a day, where he was interacting with "green" and "yellow" actors, I could see the coin drop as he realised that his communication style was awful for the people on his team who were predominantly in those camps. Of course, as a leader he wanted to make his whole team feel good and feel heard. This exercise highlighted how he could achieve that for different people.

Chapter 7: Leadership Team

Recommended tools for psychometric testing

- **Team Management Survey (TMS)**
  Developed by Margerison-McCann, TMS identifies individual work preferences and maps them to team roles for better collaboration. I've personally used this tool for 25 years.

- **Insights® Discovery**
  Based on Carl Jung's psychological theories it uses colour-coded personality types to provide insight, communication and self-awareness.

- **Myers-Briggs Type Indicator (MBTI)**
  MBTI is popular as it is well tailored to individual analysis. It assesses personality preferences and how individuals perceive the world and make decisions. However, for leadership team development I recommend looking at others that go deeper into leadership team dynamics.

- **DISC Personality Assessment**
  DISC measures dominance, influence, steadiness and conscientiousness to analyse workplace interactions. It's an easy-to-understand framework for behavioural tendencies.

- **Hogan Personality Inventory (HPI)**
  HPI evaluates personality traits important for job performance, leadership potential and team fit. It's also highly validated for professional use.

- **CliftonStrengths (formerly StrengthsFinder)**
  Developed by Gallup, it identifies and leverages individuals' top talents for personal and professional growth. It's light and easier to carry out for the public, not exclusive to professional use.

- **16 Personality Factors Questionnaire (16PF)**
  This analyses 16 personality traits relevant for career planning, team roles and leadership. It's well-suited for detailed psychological profiling.

Fun fact: My first professional rejection from a large Fortune 500 company as a young engineer came down to me not fitting into one of the 16 personality traits.

What we've noticed is many of the companies that we've worked with that have surpassed all their goals for growth use these kinds of tools to help them with every hiring decision. They will either ask us to run the tests on candidates they're considering, or in some cases they will invest in training someone in their HR team to be able to use the tools and do it in-house.

Chapter 7:
Leadership Team

These high-growth businesses don't have time to "storm and norm" to see where someone might fit – they want to make the best possible hiring decision every time. These companies are probably in the top quartile of businesses.

Many companies in the mid quartiles will probably revisit these tools every two to three years. Sometimes they'll rerun testing when a certain percentage of their workforce has changed. Others will incorporate it into a team day.

We also find that around one-third of people will make use of the online tools to help them learn more about their strengths and weaknesses, and to build on their weaknesses, but this often depends on the leader.

Succession planning for executive teams

Often succession planning is thought of as optional, even though most people who are in executive leadership positions have been to business school and objectively understand that the cost of losing someone is quite high. As I write this, I believe succession planning is more critical now than ever before, because the rate of change and movement is so fast.

I will often force my clients to consider their succession plans each quarter because this is so critical to their business success. Too many times I've seen a business that already has gaps in its team lose a key person and then take a much bigger hit than they would have if they had just thought about this sooner.

So, how do you succession-plan properly? Ideally, you carry out this exercise on a three-year timeline. This gives you a bit of a runway because you can see that you have gaps under some of your key positions. With that runway, you would potentially make choices to bring people in at a higher level the next time you're hiring, with a view that they could fill that gap.

The problem is, if you're not looking then you won't see the gap until the last minute. At that point, it will probably be too expensive to bring in the person you need as a backup for a key member of your leadership team. In my opinion, leaders should be looking to fill at least 80 per cent of their gaps with a backup, and to do that effectively you need a two- to three-year timeline.

Succession planning doesn't have to be complicated. It is as simple as looking at your organisational chart, identifying the key positions within it and working out how far away other members of your team are from filling those positions. If you discover they are too far away, you mark that position with a red dot and you make a plan.

In some cases, someone else within the organisation might be able to cover that position for, let's say, three

Chapter 7:
Leadership Team

months while you hire into that role. This is a viable solution, particularly in a high-growth company where you can't necessarily afford to have someone at that level ready and waiting to take over.

Of course, there are some positions that are absolutely critical and there needs to be a plan for who would cover them in the event of a sudden absence. The CEO is one role that you need a strong succession plan for, as an example.

It's not enough to just create a succession plan and file it away. You need to review this plan every three months. You can also use this as leverage to hire people who are of a higher level. When you do this well, you're ideally looking to potentially replace yourself with a new hire.

Many people find this approach intimidating and worry about potentially bringing in someone who is better than them. However, if you fail to plan for your own succession as an executive, you risk holding the whole business back. Ideally, each hire you make should be someone who at the very least has the acumen to make it to that level, even if they aren't quite there yet.

Advice for new CEOs to get the right team in place

When you step into the CEO role, there are three key things to do in your first month in the job to ensure you have the right executive team around you.

1. Use one of the psychometric testing tools I've shared to help you open up the conversation and to understand the holistic makeup of your current team.

2. Invest time in getting to know each member of your team one-on-one. Have casual conversations with them, but also prepare a set list of questions so you can assess how each member of your executive team reacts differently to them. Without consistent questions, you can have conversations but you can't easily compare each team member

   Examples of questions you can ask are: How satisfied are you that you'll be able to hit your numbers this year? How satisfied are you that you've got a good understanding of all of your markets? How satisfied are you with your team?

   The reason I use the word "satisfied" is that it avoids you being critical, and means you don't have to ask questions like, "How could you improve your

Chapter 7:
Leadership Team

team?" but you'll likely get insights about potential improvements.

3. Ask each member of your executive team to give a short presentation about their division within the first three weeks of your tenure. We call this a storyboard, but really it is just a simple structured format of ten slides that each executive can use to give an overview of their division. I would expect anyone at this level to have enough material to be able to put this kind of presentation together relatively quickly and easily.

Once you have got a strong leadership in place, and you know how you want to build on your base to deliver step-out growth, the next step is communicating the strategic change to everyone in your organisation.

Strategic Copilot
A CEO's Guide to Changing Times

Chapter 8

Communicating Strategic Change

In the consulting model myself and my team use, communication comes second only to establishing the strong foundation – your base – that I've discussed in the previous chapters.

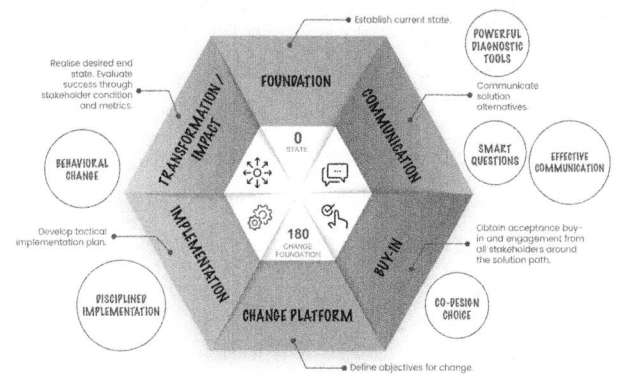

Haig Barrett Consulting Model

The reason communication is the next step on this model is that communication barriers are one of the biggest challenges to creating a successful leadership team. In fact, a survey found 44 per cent of executives say that communication barriers cause delays or failure to complete projects.[21]

Part of establishing your base involves creating a foundational message of where you are. Once you understand where you are, we tend to introduce the concept of multiperspectivity. This means that you don't just want to tell the story from your own, one-dimensional perspective, but that you want to consider how other people might see what you're doing.

It can be helpful to brainstorm with your executive team and your Board here. It can also help to work with a team like mine who can ask really smart questions and help you uncover all the angles. Once you're confident you can cover all the perspectives with your story, the next stage is to get buy-in for the strategy you've created.

In Chapter 5 I shared some tips for creating alignment within your team, one of which was to take the time to speak to each person individually before finalising the plan

---

21 McKinsey & Company (2022) "Leading Off: Communicating more effectively: A leader's guide" Available at: https://www.mckinsey.com/~/media/mckinsey/email/leadingoff/2022/05/02/2022-05-02b.html.

Chapter 8:
Communicating Strategic Change

with everyone in the room. This is one of the most effective ways to get buy-in because you're gaining acceptance by engagement. In some cases, you may co-design the eventual solution, which also helps generate buy-in because everyone feels ownership over the final plan.

From here, you can then move through the remaining stages of the model: the final plan that you've created is your change platform. Once you have this, you can clearly define the obstacles to change, and then you're ready to move forward and consider implementation.

This is when you develop a tactical implementation plan. If you've already carried out leadership assessments and acted on what you learnt, you'll know you have the right people onboard. If you don't have the right people, you need to hire them. This could mean bringing in a consulting firm, hiring a project manager specifically for this change project or hiring an entire team.

Once you have the right people in place you can implement your tactical plan. Finally, you move into the last stage of the model: transformation impact. This is where you ensure that the right behavioural changes are happening in each of your divisions. As I mentioned earlier, around one-third of your employees will completely buy into what you're doing and these people will be the catalyst that drives change forward in your organisation.

You can even appoint specific change ambassadors within that third of your employees, who are rewarded for helping bring others onboard with the strategy. You always work your way down from the people who are most engaged in the change to those who are least engaged. Don't spend your time or energy trying to convince the bottom third of people that the change is good.

Instead, focus on that top third who can help bring people sitting in the middle onboard too. As they understand what is happening and that an initiative is positive for the company, they will also buy into the strategy. Then you have to watch the third that doesn't really want to change.

In my experience it's best to leave it to their own managerial line managers to keep them on track. You might offer rewards or even give them the opportunity to develop a project they're passionate about on the condition that they play ball with the wider strategy for the whole organisation. As you bring everyone around to the change, you get the transformation impact you're looking for, and then you can start the whole process again.

Listen and observe

As a CEO, it can feel challenging to become an observer of your own company, but when you are able to find

Chapter 8:
Communicating Strategic Change

a level of detachment, to listen and observe, you will learn a great deal. One of the strengths I bring to all the companies I work with is not being attached to a specific outcome. I encourage all the CEOs I work with to cultivate this same mindset.

When you initially talk to people about the new strategy, it's important that you are very open and also that you don't react negatively to what you hear. You can't show a lot of emotion about what's being said, even if it's something you disagree with, because otherwise you shut down the conversation. The goal is to observe and to listen.

A concept that I like to embody is the idea of being alien, by which I mean you don't make assumptions about the responses you are expecting. You have to put yourself in a position where you don't rely on any knowledge you think you already have and instead simply listen. This all ties in with developing a multi-perspective view of the problem or the solution that you've brought to that problem. What might others see that you don't?

You want to hear the opinions that are on the edge of your perspective, because these could lead to your next big idea. Just look at the Haier example I shared earlier in the book to see the difference that listening can make.

Understand other communication styles

In the previous chapter I shared an overview of the Insights® psychometric testing tool. This can be useful to understand how you may need to modify your communication style to suit others on your executive team.

The following is a diagram showing how the different profiles of those within a team could be represented on a wheel. There is a lot of discussion in business these days about diversity, and what this shows is diversity in terms of people's communication styles and how they like to be communicated to.

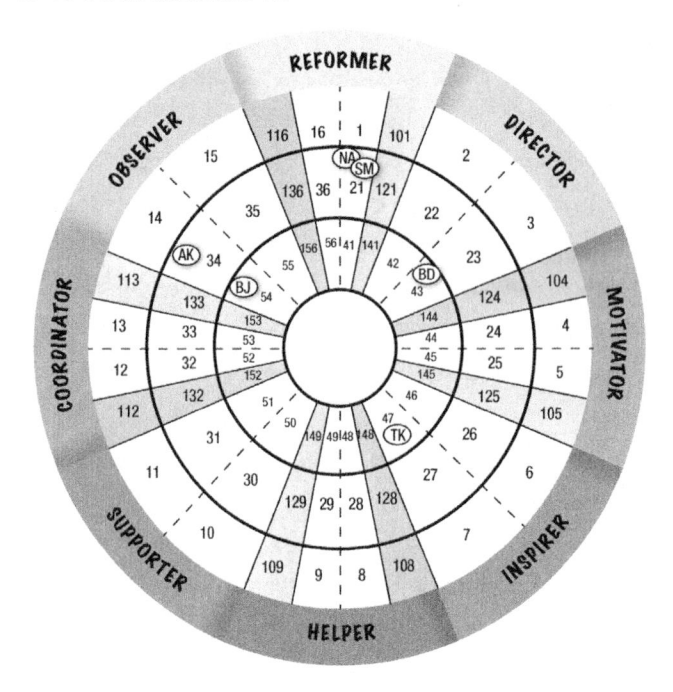

Chapter 8:
Communicating Strategic Change

Carl Jung once said that everything that irritates us about others can lead us to a better understanding of ourselves. This tool can help us to do that. Although the wheel shows a spectrum of colours, broadly the Insights® tool deals with four main colours – red, yellow, green and blue – as I described in the previous chapter.

In terms of communication, we can break down these four main types as follows:

- Red seeks security and control. They want to maintain success and are all about leadership and competitiveness. In communication they are often brief and can be irritated by inefficiency and indecision. They are very quick and decisive.
- Yellow seeks security and flexibility. They are all about relationships. They want to maintain their status, can be more playful than reds and they want to be in a stimulating environment. They are likely to be outgoing, are often extroverted in nature and want to be admired. They're irritated by boredom and routine, and their decisions tend to be spontaneous.
- Green is also big on relationships and wants support. They want warmth and for everyone on the team to feel comfortable. They value loyalty and like to conform. When it comes to communication they value pleasant interactions and want everyone to be able to have their say.

They are irritated by insensitivity and impatience. Their decisions are usually quite considered.

- Blue seeks preparation and security. They won't want to make a quick decision. Instead they will want to look at data and carry out analysis before deciding anything. They want to maintain their credibility and achieve acceptance through correctness and thoroughness. They value precision and are irritated by surprises and unpredictability. Their decisions are paced and deliberate.

Just by reading those descriptions you can already imagine how a red leader pushing for a decision to be made by the end of a meeting could be incompatible with blue and green members of the team who value having more time to think about, discuss and analyse a situation before making a decision.

You might wonder how this diversity can benefit a business. The key is to teach those on the leadership team how to communicate together in a fashion that works for all of them, so that this diversity can be harnessed to deliver a truly high-performing team. One of the things we do with our clients is train them to consider the different ways in which people operate and consider how they can accommodate everyone's preferences.

Chapter 8:
Communicating Strategic Change

This might mean training someone who is predominantly red to set up a meeting brief a week before a big strategy meeting, to give the blues time to prepare. If a lot of new ideas come out of that meeting, then a green or yellow who is leading the meeting might suggest breaking and reconvening in two days to give the blues time to do some further research and gather their thoughts.

If you were to let someone who is red lead the meeting, they might push for an immediate answer, which wouldn't allow everyone to contribute to their full potential. It would likely also mean that the organisation could be missing key information or insights that will be gathered through research. Of course, you can't take too long to make a decision, so a lot of this work is about finding the right balance.

Much of the work we do is about helping executive teams to gel, and to get them to think about how they might communicate differently, which is why we bring in actors to role-play different personality types, as I explained in the previous chapter. As a CEO, it's important that you can change the way you communicate so that you can have meaningful interactions with different people and appreciate the diversity in your broader team.

All of this work allows you to frame the conversation around change in a constructive way. When you can frame conversations around the step-out growth strategy by showing how this will benefit the whole business, it is easier to get buy-in for changes that might otherwise receive a lot of pushback.

Let's imagine that in order to step out into a new cutting-edge area of technology, you need to let ten people in the research and development (R&D) team go. Could some of them move into this new area? Would this mean they are therefore less resistant to the change because they are getting to work on an exciting new project rather than sticking with what they know?

If you talk about the need to grow into new areas as a means of protecting the business, because the core business isn't enough, it is often received more positively. This is because even if the change means job losses, everyone can understand that this will benefit the business. You need to demonstrate that this shift in strategy will help the company stay ahead of the game, and in doing so protect far more jobs than it costs.

Tools like the Insights® Discovery Wheel also allow you to see where you are falling short in your organisation. All of us will have biases when it comes to hiring, but by using tools like this we can identify what kinds of people need to be brought into a given team to give it the diversity of thought required to thrive in a fast-changing world.

Chapter 8:
Communicating Strategic Change

You need people with all of those styles to move your business forward. In the face of a black swan event, a red leader who can make instant decisions is ideal. But in other situations, taking the time to step back and analyse, as a blue leader would, can allow you to sidestep a significant challenge. However, often CEOs will hire people in their own image, which means the leadership team is out of balance.

If everyone wants to come up with new ideas and attack the market, but there is no one analysing and doing the work, your business will very quickly run into problems. What this tool, and others like it, allows you to do is find the balance you need to prevent your whole top team simply chasing the next shiny thing without executing on any of it or being held accountable for their commitments.

The value of a strategic Board

When you're in transformation mode, you also want a strategic Board to support you. Not all Boards will be strategically minded though. Therefore, as the CEO, you may have to suggest bringing in new Board members who know your industry intimately or who are future-focused to help you deliver your step-out growth strategy.

In many cases, we suggest bringing in an advisory Board. This does not interfere with the Board itself; instead it allows you to pick some subject matter experts from around the world who can come to four meetings a year and help you drive some of your step-out growth.

This doesn't have to be a hugely expensive endeavour. In my experience, many people who are highly engaged and passionate about their niche enjoy the process of being part of an advisory Board and won't require huge financial sums to be involved. Everyone wants to be part of innovation and success. They want to have their finger on the pulse of positive market initiatives within their industry or area of expertise.

Having the right steering team in place can be the difference between a project maintaining momentum and staying on track, or falling behind schedule and out of scope. We worked closely with one Louisiana-based company to set up a steering team for their change initiative. What was interesting in this situation was that two people who would not have been included on the steering team without our input went on to become some of the most critical members of that team.

One of those was the Chief Information Officer (CIO). The CEO felt that the technology requirement for this project was elementary, but the CIO's input turned out to be invaluable.

Chapter 8:
Communicating Strategic Change

The other thing we did in this particular instance was fix dates for monthly meetings nine months in advance. We had a set agenda for each so that all of those involved knew exactly what they would need to make decisions about and when.

This prevented one of the most common challenges that I see in corporate initiatives, which is senior leaders sending people who don't have the authority to make decisions to sit in for them in meetings. Because everyone on the steering team was engaged, and stuck to their commitment of showing up for every meeting, we had great success with this particular project.

Managing communication barriers

According to research from the *Open Journal of Business and Management*, different communication styles are the cause of 34.8 per cent of communication barriers in the workplace.[22] The second most common reason for communication barriers is conflict, which accounts for 29.3 per cent of barriers.

---

22   *Open Journal of Business and Management*, Vol.9 No.2, March 2021. Available at: https://www.scirp.org/journal/paperinformation?paperid=107818&

It's important to point out that you're never going to completely remove conflict from your team, because no team will be perfect. However, if you have done the work around putting the right team in place that I've already discussed in this book, you will have fewer conflict-based communication issues than you otherwise would have. The conflicts you do have will also likely be resolved more quickly thanks to the foundations you've laid for your team.

The other main barriers to communication identified by this research are lack of transparency and trust, an inability to listen to others, cultural differences and various perceptions. In my experience, many of these can be solved by using the tools I'm sharing with you in this book. The key is for whoever is leading meetings where conflict arises to bring the team together and use such tools to guide the conversation and ensure it remains constructive.

It takes a great deal of skill to use these tools properly to bring harmony to a group, and this is something I think many CEOs underestimate. It's crucial to create a psychologically safe space for everyone on the team – or what I like to call a sacred space – where everyone feels like they can say anything. This is another time when an outside facilitator like myself can be incredibly valuable, because I don't have any of the history with the other

Chapter 8:
Communicating Strategic Change

people in the room that might make it difficult for me to remain unbiased and create a sacred space.

How communication affects organisational performance

There has been a lot of research into how unconscious bias and blind spots affect organisational performance. The way I see communication is that not understanding how you prefer to communicate, and how those around you prefer to communicate, is another blind spot that, as a CEO, you need to address.

This is no different to working on removing any other blind spots you have. For example, I know that I am quite conservative and my unconscious bias is not to take risks. When I realised that I was quite antifailure, I acknowledged that this could hold me back as a leader, so I filled my advisory Board with people who could balance that.

As a result, when I was blocked and thinking that it wasn't worth taking a risk, but felt that it was close to looking good, I would take the opportunity to my advisers to get their opinion. If two or three of my advisers told me that what I was looking at was a moderate risk, and that in their opinion they would take it, then I would go ahead.

Because of this approach, I've had some huge successes with my business that I otherwise would have missed. I've moved into industries that I wouldn't otherwise have; I've grown my US business substantially and I moved back to the UK, all because I acknowledged my blind spot and sought to diversify my thinking.

The way in which communication is used within an organisation can have a significant impact on its performance. When people are encouraged to be open and honest, to debate and have a clear exchange of ideas, they reduce misunderstandings and increase efficiency. By contrast, when communication is overly aggressive or passive, it has the opposite effect and increases conflict, reduces morale and decreases productivity.

The need to listen

You can't communicate unless you listen, that's the honest truth. Communication – particularly about strategy and change – is about the other person, not about you. This comes back to the theme of multiperspectivity, in that you need to hear things from other points of view and other perspectives to be in a position to consider all the angles and spot opportunities.

This can certainly be a challenge, but I would urge you to find a way to turn off that voice in the back of your head

Chapter 8:
Communicating Strategic Change

that is telling you what you think you're going to hear. One of the three most critical traits of being a trusted adviser, according to David Maister, is the ability to listen and understand what people are saying.

Not everyone is a natural listener. If we go back to the four main insight profiles, you could generalise and say that perhaps a red leader might not always be good at listening to everyone around them. This doesn't necessarily mean that the red leader needs to change their behaviour, but my advice would be to ensure they have someone they trust on their team who is a strong green. This green person is then able to stand up and say, "You need to listen to this person, because ..." and for the red leader to take that onboard.

Listening is a skill, and certainly one that you can train yourself to get better at. A large part of becoming a better communicator is being aware of your natural communication style, understanding where you need support and finding the right people to provide that support.

Connecting communication with decision-making

Your communication style will have an impact on your decision-making process, and this in turn will naturally have an impact on the speed at which you make decisions.

This affects the speed with which you can move forward with new strategies and react to your competitors.

In today's world, speed counts for a lot. Many of the clients we work with who have achieved amazing success and are part of high-performing teams are able to make decisions within hours, rather than spending days or even weeks going back and forth before deciding what to do.

The reason they are able to make decisions so quickly is because they have an excellent understanding of the people on their teams. They are therefore able to put the right people in the room for an hour and for that meeting to result in the right decision. Making sure that decision-makers are sitting down together is critical – as soon as the people in a meeting need to get approval from their boss before an initiative can move forward, you create drag and slow the whole process down.

Chapter 8:
Communicating Strategic Change

Spotlight on Brian O'Keefe

Role: Corporate Storyteller, Articulus LLC

Tenure: March 2006–present

Biggest strengths: Helping people find the heart of their message and communicating that with others.

Achievements: Leaving engineering behind to become a corporate storytelling coach, where he's helped hundreds of people learn to communicate in a more engaging way.

Brian O'Keefe spoke to me about the importance of framing in decision-making when we spoke on the *Other Side of the Business Card* podcast. To frame a story effectively, you need four things:

Strategic Copilot
A CEO's Guide to Changing Times

1. Something to grab their attention and make them interested.

2. A way to get the other person engaged and involved in the conversation.

3. Something that they can learn. You need to teach them something.

4. To equip them with information to make a decision.

> "One of the most important things to do in your job is help other people make decisions, and I think it's also one of the most difficult parts of our jobs. This is true whether we're talking to a co-worker, management, a partner of ours or a customer. Helping someone make a decision isn't easy because a lot of times you already have it formulated in your head. You have an opinion of how things should work. And the question is, other than just telling them what you think, is there a way to tell them what you think but in a way that helps them arrive at the same conclusion as you? Or if they don't agree with you, to reach a place where they better understand what you're

Chapter 8:
Communicating Strategic Change

> saying so that you can have a more productive conversation?"[23]

Brian explained that our brains need the four steps outlined earlier in order to make a decision based on what you're sharing with them. You need to capture their attention, engage them in the conversation, teach them something new and then share the information they need to make a decision.

> "Our founder at Articulus used to like to say: 'I don't believe you can convince anyone to do anything. What I do believe is, if you give people the right information in the right way, they can convince themselves.' That's always stuck with me. Corporate storytelling is a process by which you can share what you consider to be the right information in the right way.
>
> I've always tried to take that approach. So, I'm not trying to convince them, I'm just trying to give them the right information in the right way. And then I want them to convince themselves, either in the moment or after I've gone."

---

23 *Other Side of the Business Card*, Brian O'Keefe (December 2022). Available at: https://www.haigbarrettpartners.com/the-other-side-of-the-business-card/episode/37f01d1f/s2e5-or-the-power-of-corporate-storytelling-with-brian-okeefe.

Strategic Copilot
A CEO's Guide to Changing Times

When you can frame the information and the decision in the right way, the end result is better, faster, more accurate decision-making that leads to accelerated business growth. This is the power that corporate storytelling can have.

In the 21st century, leaders often don't have the luxury of time. The speed with which the world around us changes is significantly faster than it has been at any point, certainly in recent human history. Making quick, mostly right, decisions is only one part of the puzzle. You also need to develop the right skills to allow you to handle rapid change and make pivots within your organisation.

To access additional resources around the theme of preparing for and staying on track with transformation, scan the following QR code:

The Speed of Change

As we've discussed already, the speed with which change happens as I write this is far beyond anything we've experienced in the past. Gone are the days when a five-year plan has value. I usually don't advise my clients to look more than three years into the future, and even then there's a fair chance that after 12 months everything will look materially different from what we thought.

For CEOs, rapid change presents challenges and opportunities. It can be hard to plan and allocate resources when things are in such a constant state of flux. But it can also open up doors that lead to significant step-out growth if you walk through them at the right time.

Strategic Copilot
A CEO's Guide to Changing Times

What we'll explore in this part of the book are the traits you can develop and tools you can use to help you and your organisation thrive in this fast-changing environment.

Chapter 9

Being Agile

Agility in business is the ability to, at times, enact radical change. At others, agility is about simply making smaller adjustments to the likes of your supply chain or products based on some of the signals you see in the world and environment around you.

For example, three months before the Covid-19 pandemic gripped the world, some organisations saw issues building in China. An example of agility in this context might have been shipping products out of Wuhan a month earlier than they otherwise would have. That isn't a significant pivot, but it is a minor adjustment that allows your business to stay ahead of the curve.

One of my clients had a huge international expansion plan, but when the Covid-19 pandemic hit in 2020, they immediately pivoted away from that. They were able to do so quickly and with confidence because they had mapped out their five futures, which I talked about in Chapter 6. They were able to choose the most appropriate of their plan Bs and that made the business agile enough that it could pivot without suffering too much.

One person who has done this incredibly well throughout his career is John Nicols, who now acts as a strategic adviser for Codexis having retired from the role of CEO.

Spotlight on John Nicols

Role: Board Director and Adviser to biotech CEOs, CEO and Owner of Organicols, LLC, Former President & CEO; Board Member, Codexis Inc

Tenure: June 2012–August 2022

Chapter 9: Being Agile

> **Biggest strengths:** Ability to deliver sustained growth and value creation across diverse global businesses. Relentless focus on team, financials, product development, marketing and technological innovation as a leader.
>
> **Achievements:** Positioning Codexis as a leader in protein-based innovations for various industries. Turned around Albemarle's struggling half-a-billion-dollar fine chemicals business and globalised the company's flame retardants business.

When we spoke on the *Other Side of the Business Card*, John and I talked about how he had lived in various places throughout his working life, including Tokyo, and I learnt that his move to Asia was by design.

"I lobbied the company I was working for at the time (Albemarle) to send me to Tokyo because we wanted to get ahead of the trends in Asia. We're talking about the early 90s, when the business was involved in plastic additives for flame-retardant chemicals. But these additives are required for making electronics products like circuit boards and computer cabinetry. Asia was taking over the world's manufacturing of these kinds of products, so the company allowed me to go there and focus on the Asian markets for our products.

Initially, they had me based in Louisiana, and for the first year I travelled like crazy to Tokyo, Singapore and even China. Ultimately, I told the leadership at the business that if they were serious about this market, that we needed to be based out there.

This was the first time I started to lead over a large organisation. I led the global flame retardant business and then I ultimately led Albemarle's half-a-billion-dollar fine chemicals business."[24]

How agile leaders operate

John's story is an example of how agile leaders see opportunities on the horizon and do what they can to steer their organisation in the right direction.

In many ways, agile leaders are like the captains of large ships – they need to anticipate and move early. Things

---

24 *Other Side of the Business Card*, John Nicols (October 2021). Available at: https://www.haigbarrettpartners.com/the-other-side-of-the-business-card/episode/411435ab/the-mindset-of-a-high-growth-ceo-with-john-nicols-president-and-chief-executive-officer-of-codexis.

are changing around them all the time. There are storms, then there are undercurrents of change. A good captain will read the weather and conditions around them, as well as looking at weather forecasts and other data to plot a preferred course, but with the understanding that they might need to deviate from this slightly. An agile CEO is no different.

They will not only have four alternatives to their preferred route mapped out. They will be able to think through each of them and the circumstances that might lead them to pivot to one or the other before those things occur.

Jon Rawding, who you met in Chapter 3, and his organisation Euro Mechanical, is an example of where the Five-Futures model was used to great effect. Jon became CEO of Euro Mechanical in 2018, and was tasked with restructuring the company. As part of that work, he brought together an agile executive team and they created their five futures. The lower growth futures were based on a black swan event.

Then in 2020 we had that black swan – the pandemic. Jon and his team were able to pivot towards one of their plan Bs seamlessly because they knew how that future would look. They couldn't possibly have predicted the global pandemic, but they had been able to think about how the business might need to restructure in the event that the global economy was completely disrupted.

The other key to being agile is diversification, as John Nicols explained during our chat on my podcast. When he joined Codexis Inc., the business had been successful for ten years, during which time it had developed incredible protein engineering technology, as you heard in Chapter 2. However, as John explained, the business had targeted creating enzymes to break down waste materials from crops to create ethanol that could be used for transportation fuel, and this wasn't a viable direction in which to go.

> "At the time the business started going in this direction, it seemed like an imperative, but the world changed dramatically and so that business went away for the world, and for Codexis. My first two years [as CEO] were about redirecting and restructuring the company, which was very difficult.
>
> The obvious lesson that came out of this was diversification. What enabled Codexis to survive is that we were doing more than just biofuels. Three-quarters of the company was focused on biofuels, but the other quarter was focused on the needs of pharmaceutical companies. Even with that limited diversification, it allowed Codexis to have two bets. When one didn't work out, we came back to the other.

As attractive as one big opportunity can be, it's very risky, so hedge some bets, especially if you're a platform technology and you're pretty early to market."

Balancing process and agility

Workflows and processes are important, but when they are embedded too rigidly, they can hold a company back from being agile and they prevent others in the organisation from being agile to changing circumstances. The key to avoiding this is to have processes driven by people, not people driven by processes.

To achieve this balance, you need to give your teams autonomy and you need to take the shackles off of everyone in the organisation. In doing so, you allow yourself as CEO, and others who work for you, to become more entrepreneurial in their approach, which supports agility.

The military is a good example of how you can blend strict processes with agility. We all know that any military organisation has strict processes in place, but there will be situations when small teams are given the freedom to do what is necessary to survive and complete their mission. They will still be operating within the embedded culture of the military organisation of which they are a part, but with the flexibility to make decisions on the ground in response to rapidly changing circumstances.

In modern organisations the need for agility is paramount. In fact, we need to embrace a paradigm shift in how we run our organisations to survive in the future. However, this can be difficult given the path we've followed since industrialisation.

In the last almost 200 years since industrialisation, we have learned and been taught through being able to measure as much as possible. Thanks to technology and decades of operating in this way, we have become good at measuring many aspects of a business' operations. Through measurement we have achieved fantastic productivity improvements on the manufacturing floor, in logistics etc.

However, when you're in a hurry to make decisions but you've automated a lot of the stuff around you that is, by definition, dependent on measurement, you realise that you can't measure everything. That is a huge problem for the future in which we need to be more agile, because we have locked ourselves into dependencies on processes and plans.

Therefore, future leaders must be able to put processes under people, rather than have processes leading people. In the end, you have to take a leap of faith, especially

Chapter 9: Being Agile

when you're in a hurry. With the life cycles of products reducing and uncertainty increasing, you have to react extremely fast.

However, many businesses aren't currently structured to react quickly, because their processes are so rigidly embedded in the way in which the business operates. This means that you have to be willing to make a major change to the way in which you lead, in order to be in a position to respond to change over existing plans. In many cases, the only way forward will be with a major change in leadership.

There are several ways in which this looks different. Firstly, you have to put the soft factors over the hard factors. Secondly, you need to have collaboration agreements with your suppliers rather than rigid contracts. Thirdly, you need to create a bridge so that you are looking forwards and not only backwards. Finally, you have to choose wisely in terms of leadership talent so you get leaders who can actually think for themselves and use the right side of their brain as much as the left side of their brain.

This means that business leaders – and therefore other stakeholders like Board members and shareholders – need to get comfortable with not having a fixed return that the business is aiming for. Instead they need to become comfortable with a range that supports agility and movement within a given plan, much like the Five-Futures model I have already shared with you.

When you can do this, you can be agile in your response to whatever changes happen in the environment within that range. We'll explore how you can support agility in your organisation, and allow your teams to become more entrepreneurial while remaining process driven, without being purely driven by process, later in this book.

Of course, agility is just one element required to navigate rapid change. Resilience is a key trait, whether in business or our personal lives, and one that the most successful CEOs actively cultivate.

Chapter 10

Resilience

Resilience is the process of adapting well in the face of adversity, perceived threat or significant sources of pressure and stress. Resilience is not a trait that people either have or do not have. It involves behaviours, thoughts and actions that anyone can learn and develop.

Every business leader, whether at the head of a large corporation or leading a small startup, needs resilience to be able to operate effectively in the VUCA (volatile, uncertain, complex, ambiguous) world in which we live and work. Since the Covid-19 pandemic, the need for resilience at every level of an organisation has only become more apparent.

American anthropologist, author and futurist Jamais Cascio coined the term BANI, which stands for brittle, anxious, nonlinear and incomprehensible. He felt that VUCA did not effectively encapsulate the rapid evolution we were experiencing in the world. BANI invites us to look at the world with a fresh perspective.

It's not necessarily that the world has become more brittle, anxious, nonlinear or incomprehensible, but that our perception of the world has shifted. As Jeroen Kraaijenbrink wrote for *Forbes*, BANI highlights how four main illusions that humanity has collectively held are now being shattered.[25] These are the illusions of strength, control, predictability and knowledge

In other words, the world has always been brittle, anxious, nonlinear and incomprehensible, and we are now beginning to accept that this is true. Of course, we also can't escape the fact that the world is changing more rapidly now than it ever has before. As leaders we have to be aware of many more factors that could influence the trajectory of our organisations than we ever have before.

---

25 Kraaijenbrink, J. (2022) "What BANI Really Means (And How It Corrects Your World View)," *Forbes*, 23 June. Available at: https://www.forbes.com/sites/jeroenkraaijenbrink/2022/06/22/what-bani-really-means-and-how-it-corrects-your-world-view/.

The need for resilience

Resilience allows us to take a multitude of factors into account when making decisions. As I write this, there is a lot of fear mongering in the media about AI and robots "taking people's jobs". But in actual fact, it is still not possible for a computer or AI to make human-like decisions in complex situations. Whether it will become possible remains to be seen.

Let's take autonomous vehicles as an example of the kind of decision I am talking about. Initially, it seems relatively simple to create a car that can drive along and avoid other vehicles. But what about if you're driving and see another car coming straight at you. You could pull to the left to avoid it, but you see what appears to be a woman with a baby in a pram who you will hit. Pull to the right and you'll hit another vehicle. You have to make a split-second decision; what do you do?

There are many nuances to that situation. Would you be more likely to survive if you swerved left, but potentially hit a woman and her child? Do you take the risk of hitting the other car and potentially suffering more severe injuries yourself as a result? There are moral dilemmas here as well as practical decisions.

What this relatively simple example illustrates is the complexity of the decision-making we have to do on a near-daily basis. When we are resilient, we are best placed to come up with responses to everything from the extreme weather we experience due to climate change, to the disruption to supply chains caused by wars.

In Chapter 7 I talked about some of the psychometric testing tools you can use to build stronger teams and better understand one another's communication styles. You can also use such tools to better understand how you deal with stress and pressure, what level of resilience you have and how you can develop it.

Stress has always been part of life. Stress in and of itself is neither good nor bad. However, being under severe stress over prolonged periods is known to have a negative impact on our physical, emotional and mental health. This doesn't just affect us on a personal level; it has business implications too.

Research shows that more than half of employees who are experiencing high levels of stress in their lives report being disengaged at work.[26] A further study found that as stress increased, productivity decreased.[27] Constantly

---

26   "Stress affecting employee engagement" (2017). Available at: https://www.hrmagazine.co.uk/content/news/stress-affecting-employee-engagement/.

27   Bui, T., Zackula, R., Dugan, K. and Ablah, E. (2021) "Workplace stress and productivity: A cross-sectional study," *Kansas Journal of Medicine*, 14. Available at: https://doi.org/10.17161/kjm.vol1413424.

stressed employees are therefore limited in their potential to be engaged, to connect with others, to communicate clearly, to undertake creative decision-making and to accept more change. To put all of this in one word, when an individual is constantly stressed, they are limited in their ability to be resilient.

Therefore, building resilience is a key skill to both improve our personal wellbeing and our effectiveness at work. Self-observation and reflection are important if we are to learn to be more resilient.

Resilience on a personal as well as an organisational level is crucial if we are to survive and thrive in the face of disruptive change and the scale of technological convergence we are experiencing.

Learning to pivot

The world is changing at a rapid pace and leaders need to find confidence in uncertainty. Climate change is one of the biggest challenges humanity faces, and it presents significant challenges for businesses too. This is not least because accepted approaches to mitigating the climate crisis are changing constantly.

Take EVs as an example. Ten to 15 years ago, EVs were billed as the future. By 2030, we would all be driving them. While EV technology has evolved and there is still a shift towards the electrification of our transportation systems as I write this, the pace at which EVs have been adopted has been much slower than originally anticipated.

Automakers have therefore had to find ways to pivot, firstly from petrol and diesel engines to EVs, and now from EVs to alternatives that meet the markets' needs. This is why we can't just plan for one future. We have to be able to see multiple versions of the future, and plan for all of them, so that we are able to pivot quickly and efficiently when required.

You can no longer create a strategic plan that only allows for one possible trajectory, as I explained at the start of this book. Instead you have to cultivate a future-thinking mindset that enables continuous adaptability.

One part of developing this mindset at a Board or senior leadership level is removing the danger of groupthink biases. You need everyone who is part of the team making strategic business decisions to feel comfortable sharing their perspectives, even if they are vastly different from the rest of the people at the table. You can't have people who want to avoid conflict keeping quiet, even though they see a risk to the strategy that no one else has spotted. This is where having a strategic facilitator can be valuable, because they can help you tease out all

Chapter 10: Resilience

of these different perspectives and discuss them in a constructive way.

One area that it has become increasingly important for executives to understand is the supply chain for their businesses. There have been so many supply chain disruptions in recent years as I write this that organisations cannot afford not to factor these into their risk analysis.

The innovation process within your organisation is also critical if you want to remain resilient. You need to have a realistic portfolio of projects, some of which are improving the efficiencies in your core business or accelerating its progress, and others which are focused on the step-out growth your business needs to move beyond your current reality.

At every stage, the innovation process needs to be carefully managed. The team steering your business innovations might change as a project moves from ideation to commercialisation to launch. You need to ensure your team also has the ability to kill a project at the right time if it's not working.

In a world that is changing so rapidly, no business can afford to continue with a project that isn't working for even six months. You don't have six months to spare in business in the 21st century. Wasting time on the wrong projects will mean you miss opportunities to start critical projects that can drive your business forward and facilitate further growth.

Even if you are working on the right projects, you might not be tackling them as efficiently as you could. It was one of the issues Tony Meggs, who you heard from in Chapter 4, identified about the Crossrail project when we spoke.

"Crossrail is too complicated. I want to stress that it's a brilliant project, with some of the best people in the world working on it, but if the UK government were to do Crossrail over again I'd tell them to simplify it at the outset. Reduce the number of interfaces, reduce the complexity. It can still be brilliant and world-class, but complexity kills."

Developing entrepreneurial resilience

Whether you love him or hate him, you can't deny that Elon Musk offers us a masterclass in entrepreneurial resilience. When you hear reports of a CEO sleeping on their office couch so that they can fix problems, alarm bells often start to ring. I certainly wouldn't recommend that any of my leadership clients start sleeping in their offices when things get tough. But that's what Musk has done in the past. And he's pulled remarkable things out of the bag.

He doesn't let go. He has ploughed through all manner of challenges at Tesla and SpaceX. Some of what those organisations have achieved is phenomenal.

The benefits entrepreneurs gain from resilience extend beyond financial success. Committing to tasks, and seeing projects through, gives leaders immeasurable lessons in business that they can leverage in future projects.

William Malek delivers workshops and classes on insights in resilience, teaching individuals how to build the skill based on their individual traits and tendencies. These sessions highlight that resilience is not an innate quality that some people possess while others do not – it is a skill that can be taught and developed.

Malek's framework highlights eight factors for building resilience:

1. **Connection:** Having caring and supportive relationships within and outside the family.

2. **Self regulation:** Maintaining the balance between too much and too little stress.

3. **Self efficacy:** Making realistic plans and taking steps to carry them out.

4. **Self care:** Making choices that promote wellbeing.

5. **Acceptance:** Seeing and accepting the reality of my situation.

6. **Meaning and purpose:** Having an overall sense of purpose and meaning.

7. **Improvising solutions:** Improvising a solution making do with whatever is at hand.

8. **Self awareness:** Knowing who you are..

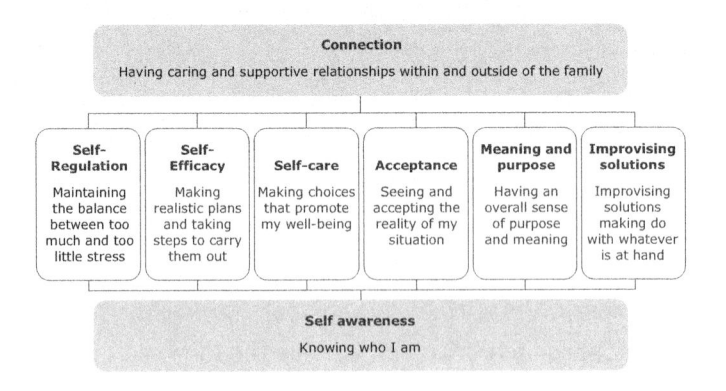

Connection — Having caring and supportive relationships within and outside of the family					
Self-Regulation	Self-Efficacy	Self-care	Acceptance	Meaning and purpose	Improvising solutions
Maintaining the balance between too much and too little stress	Making realistic plans and taking steps to carry them out	Making choices that promote my well-being	Seeing and accepting the reality of my situation	Having an overall sense of purpose and meaning	Improvising solutions making do with whatever is at hand
Self awareness — Knowing who I am					

Credit: Malek, W. (2019) *Insights® into Resilience*

As with every entrepreneurial trait discussed in this book, building resilience starts with self-awareness.

Chapter 10: Resilience

In a workshop setting, individuals are told to identify their strengths and align them with the eight factors to understand how to personally build their resilience.

By recognising that resilience is not a fixed trait but a skill that can be developed, entrepreneurs and leaders can navigate challenges more effectively, make better decisions and gain deeper insights from their experiences. The benefits of doing so are practical and will empower you to take on challenges with confidence while achieving sustainable personal growth.

To access additional resources around how to cope with the speed of change, scan the following QR code:

Strategic Copilot
A CEO's Guide to Changing Times

The Art of the Long View

In the early 21st century, the futurist and leader Peter Schwartz published *The Art of the Long View*,[28] a book dedicated to the practice and art of scenario planning. Schwartz was one of the leaders of the movement and ultimately was hired a few years after the book publication to be a senior vice-president at Salesforce.com. Scenario planning was a means to project and look forward into the immediate future. It was also a way to "see forward" by inference, and alongside other techniques could be used to make "market forward" business decisions that proved highly accurate.

---

28 Schwartz, P. (2012) *The Art of the Long View: Planning for the Future in an Uncertain World*. Crown Currency.

Strategic Copilot
A CEO's Guide to Changing Times

As we've discussed already, the "old" methods of scenario planning are no longer fit for purpose in our VUCA and BANI world. Things are changing too quickly. Black swan events are becoming more prevalent. Being tied to one possible vision of the future is too rigid.

While it is impossible to predict the future, when you head up an organisation you have to try. After all, without any foresight you can't make plans for even a few months into the future, let alone investments that will last years.

This is why CEOs have to find new ways of future planning and develop their strategic foresight to enable them to lead and have confidence, even when surrounded by uncertainty.

Chapter 11

Future Planning

The challenge with future planning as I write this book is that the world has never been so uncertain. We are in a period of great instability. These are times when more and more of us are expecting the unexpected, while simultaneously being unable to predict what form that unexpected event will take.

What does the future look like?

In the aftermath of the global pandemic and the Russian invasion of Ukraine, the World Economic Forum (WEF) published its annual Global Risks Report 2023. It characterised the coming decade by low growth and low cooperation, resulting in difficult trade-offs that can compromise climate action, human development and future resilience.[29] These themes continued in its Global Risks Report 2024.

According to the WEF, in the short term, global risks are dominated by the rising cost of living. Climate action failure looms large over the next decade. In 2023, the world experienced record-breaking heat conditions, drought, wildfires and flooding. Conflicts in Sudan, Gaza, Israel and Lebanon have only served to demonstrate how fragile the notion of world peace really is.

Over half of those surveyed for the 2024 report (54 per cent) anticipate a moderate risk of global catastrophes in the next two years. A further 30 per cent expect more extreme disruption.[30]

The Covid-19 pandemic was one such global catastrophe that no one saw coming. The economic outcome of the pandemic, alongside the conflict in Ukraine and supply chain decoupling, led to soaring inflation, a shift towards stricter monetary policies and a low-growth, low-investment era. Governments and central banks will face persistent inflationary pressures. There's also a

---

29   World Economic Forum (no date) "Global Risks Report 2023". Available at: https://www.weforum.org/publications/global-risks-report-2023/digest/.
30   World Economic Forum (no date) "Global Risks Report 2024". Available at: https://www.weforum.org/publications/global-risks-report-2024/digest/.

looming risk of a misalignment between monetary and fiscal policies, potentially triggering liquidity shocks and a protracted economic downturn, alongside the challenge of supply-driven inflation.

Economic warfare is becoming more common. We're seeing increasing clashes between global powers and state intervention in markets. The WEF predicts economic policies will be used defensively, to build self-sufficiency and sovereignty from rival powers, as well as offensively to constrain the rise of others. This geoeconomic weaponisation raises concerns about escalating distrust and decoupling in globally integrated economies. The outcome will be inefficiencies and higher prices.

According to the WEF, the longer-term risk landscape could be marked by multidomain conflicts and asymmetric warfare with the deployment of new-tech weaponry on a potentially more destructive scale.

Technology will exacerbate inequalities. Cybersecurity threats will persist. Prompted by state aid and military expenditure, as well as private investment, development of emerging technologies will yield advancements in AI, quantum computing and biotechnology, among other technologies. These technologies will provide partial solutions to a range of emerging crises, from healthcare to food security and climate mitigation. But they also bring risks, from widening misinformation and disinformation to unmanageably rapid churn in both blue- and white-collar jobs.

Environmental risks dominated the current, two-year and ten-year risk landscapes in the 2024 report. The gap between necessary climate action and political feasibility is widening. This is hampering progress on climate action. Compounding crises are impacting societies more broadly, contributing to a global cost-of-living crisis. Food, fuel and cost crises exacerbate societal vulnerability. Declining investments in human development erode future resilience.

Concurrent shocks, deeply interconnected risks and eroding resilience are giving rise to the risk of polycrises. This is a situation where different crises interact such that the overall impact far exceeds the sum of each part.

This might all sound bleak. But this is the reality of the world we face as I write this in 2024. In our globalised world, organisations cannot escape or insulate themselves fully from shocks that happen elsewhere in the world. The domino effect from one event can be significant. One example is the supply chain disruption that arose following Russia's invasion of Ukraine, but there are many more.

How to prepare for future shocks

According to the WEF, the way to shape a more secure future is through more effective preparedness. We may not know what crisis, or crises, are coming our way, but we can put ourselves in a position to adapt when they do.

This is where scenario planning comes into its own. Many organisations already use scenario planning for navigating the risks that they can, in one way or another, see coming. But leaders today need to be able to plan for future shocks that are beyond their foresight.

The themes we discussed in the Speed of Change section of this book are key – being agile, resilience, and embracing AI and digital transformation.

In their book *Radical Uncertainty*, prominent British economists John Kay and Mervyn King suggest that we should embrace uncertainty by adopting robust, adaptable strategies and narratives to address alternative futures and unforeseeable events.[31] In the 21st century, they stress this is more effective than using probability calculations to fill the gaps in our knowledge.

---

31 King, M. and Kay, J. (2020) *Radical Uncertainty: Decision-making for an Unknowable Future.* Hachette UK.

Their concept of "radical uncertainty" focuses on the vast spectrum of possibilities that exist between improbable events. This realm encompasses uncertain futures and unpredictable outcomes. It is one where speculation is essential and disagreements often remain unresolved. In practical terms, this is the world we frequently navigate. It encompasses both individual and collective decisions, as well as those in the realms of finance, economics and politics.

Effective decision-making in the face of "radical uncertainty" demands a diverse skill set, which is rarely possessed by a single individual. Instead, decision-making in today's world thrives through collaborative processes, collective intelligence and judgement.

Based on the work I do with my clients, I agree with their assessment of what's required to navigate through such uncertain times. We need to hear various perspectives to help us more fully comprehend the situation at hand. As a leader, it is your job to ensure those perspectives are heard and carefully considered.

Scenario planning in an uncertain age

We can still find value and insights in the scenario planning models that we have used in the past. However, we have to recognise their limitations and ensure we seek the broader context in which the challenges we face sit.

We also have to be prepared to be blindsided by crises that were beyond our foresight. The key is not to plan for specific scenarios, but instead to develop flexible long-term strategies that can adapt to any shocks that occur.

One study, published in the *Harvard Business Review* in 2022, explored how Nordic companies in particular evolved their decision-making and scenario models in response to novel risks.[32] Novel risks are defined as risks stemming from unforeseen, complex combinations of seemingly routine events or familiar events occurring on an unprecedented scale and pace.

For this study, researchers interviewed over 40 top leaders from 14 global businesses across various Nordic countries. These organisations spanned sectors such as air travel, industrial manufacturing and consumer-facing industries. The study coincided with the Covid-19 Omicron variant's resurgence and Russia's invasion of Ukraine. Many of these Nordic firms had substantial operations in Russia, and all were significantly affected by factors such as energy prices.

---

32 Heikkinen, K., Kerr, W., Malin, M., Routila, P. and Rupponen, E. (2023) "When Scenario Planning Fails." Available at: https://hbr.org/2023/04/when-scenario-planning-fails.

When discussing novel risks, the leaders in question frequently used terms like "ambiguous" and "unclear". This lack of clarity made it challenging to define critical parameters for scenario development and rendered the traditional scenario planning method impractical.

However, despite the challenge, they adapted scenario planning to their new reality. The research team grouped these insights into four levels.

Level 1: Expanding scenario horizons

Unsurprisingly, most leaders have broadened their scope by considering a more extensive and diverse range of scenarios. They now explore once-unthinkable events, such as invasions of their own countries or conflicts like a US–China war over Taiwan. This was the most common step, and one that is recommended for all leadership teams. After all, these are not the first wars nor is it the first pandemic we have faced.

Level 2: Vulnerabilities as a guiding prism

At a higher level, leaders have fortified their scenario planning by scrutinising its impact on critical aspects of their businesses, particularly vulnerabilities. One of the key findings here is that companies should be able to calculate the financial reserves needed to endure a three-month period at half their revenue. Some of the leaders involved in the study went on to insist worst-case scenarios are included in all divisional plans and budgets.

Being honest about all potential vulnerabilities is essential. There may be some you would prefer to overlook, such as the departure of key talent. However, these vulnerabilities can exacerbate crises and it's important to acknowledge their potential impact.

Level 3: Robust action frameworks and internal communication

Predefined actions and roles have become more pivotal than meticulously detailed scenarios. Many organisations have transitioned to employing "general guidelines for handling various scenarios" instead of attempting to outline specific scenarios and corresponding actions.

However, it is important to consider what might be needed in different contexts. For example, during a pandemic, speed at a local level was highlighted as crucial by the leaders surveyed. This meant less centralised decision-making. By contrast, a consistent, unified message – and therefore greater centralised decision-making – was required in response to the Russian invasion of Ukraine.

This was deemed essential to maintain a company's reputation.

So, creating differing guidelines based on the characteristics of a crisis is important, because one size doesn't fit all.

Level 4: Integrating crisis management into organisational structure

Most of the companies surveyed decentralised decision-making authority as part of their pandemic response, which has proven effective. In doing so, they've moved from a hierarchical management mindset to a location-based approach.

However, there was roughly a 50-50 split in how organisations approached alignment for crisis management. In one camp are those who have integrated crisis measures into existing structures and processes. This typically involved designating an executive team member to oversee the specific crisis response.

In the other camp were those organisations that formed new taskforces to address these events. Interestingly, some companies leveraged pre-existing structures and processes, creatively adapting them. For instance, one company had an established team dedicated to handling

Chapter 11: Future Planning

industry volatility, which served as the foundation for their pandemic and war response. This approach minimised the involvement of upper management in operational decisions and has become a model for managing future unexpected events. Such adaptability holds promise for companies facing novel risks in the future.

The lesson from this research, and from what I am seeing with my clients, is that scenario planning is still relevant. However, we need to recognise its limitations and practicality in an increasingly uncertain world. Rather than being the sole tool with which organisations plan for the future, scenario planning should be part of a broader toolkit.

This toolkit should complement customised plans with a more adaptable capability to discern how the characteristics of a novel risk or shock will interact with the company's vulnerabilities and strengths. Forward-thinking organisations will enhance their internal communication channels and structures to guide responses across various scenarios. While maintaining a "plan B" mentality is necessary at times, the solution isn't to improve the accuracy of our predictions of an inherently uncertain future. Instead, the key lies in enhancing preparedness to effectively manage unexpected shocks.

Future-proofing and fire-proofing

Future-proofing is all about having a broader view of what situations may not go the way you think they will, and therefore having alternatives in mind. This involves what we've just discussed around new ways of scenario planning – ensuring that you have a "plan B" and that you adopt multiperspectivity in your thinking.

One thing I've encountered is a reluctance among some of my clients to consider a "plan B". However, as we've seen from the examples in this chapter, and from our own experiences in recent years, this is not advisable. We have to accept that things may not go the way we expect. Executives in today's world need to have a "plan B" for what's around every corner, along with the resilience and agility to respond to any shocks they encounter.

Fire-proofing is going through this process with your management team to ensure that they also consider multiple perspectives and have their own "plan B". You need to be confident they will make the right decisions if they are left in charge. Your executives also need to be able to develop their own teams and work autonomously if things need to change quickly.

As the CEO, you have to set the boundaries within which they can make decisions. You also need to ensure that every person on your leadership team understands what those boundaries are.

What we are seeing in the world now is a shift from command-and-control leadership within organisations to a more hybrid approach, where the collective intelligence of an executive team is crucial to the quality of the decision-making. In emergency situations, there may be a reversion to command-and-control decision-making out of necessity. However, it's crucial to develop your executive team's skills around decision-making, future-proofing, bringing together the right team in a time of crisis and leveraging their collective intelligence to arrive at the best possible decision.

All of this feeds into developing strategic foresight, both as a leader and as an organisation.

Strategic Copilot
A CEO's Guide to Changing Times

Chapter 12

Strategic Foresight

Strategic foresight involves analysing trends, signals and uncertainties to map out potential futures and guide your organisation's direction towards sustainable success.

Peter Drucker said: "The best way to predict the future is to create it."[33] In today's world, where everything is changing so quickly, this is more true than ever. In the past, a company could look at what had happened in the business previously, see what had already worked and put a lot of oomph into that. This would usually be spot on to drive them into the future and towards growth.

---

33 Cohen, W.A. (2009) *Drucker on Leadership: New Lessons from the Father of Modern Management.* John Wiley & Sons.

Strategic Copilot
A CEO's Guide to Changing Times

The world doesn't work like this any more. Things don't just change year by year, they change month by month, week by week and, in some cases, day by day. A three-year strategy will very often end up outdated by the time you reach the end of year one, let alone year three.

Strategic foresight allows you to run your business based on the future, not on the past. For example, an industrial company that wants to deliver organic growth could use strategic foresight to help them understand to what degree higher risk-reward opportunities are available if they want to take their products to a wider market. Taking a strategic approach to the future will also allow the company to understand the future to the extent that they could find balance between monetising for the long term and bringing in money on a shorter time frame.

In some cases, this approach may also help the company better understand where they want to use partners, if at all. It can also help them develop an execution strategy for the expansion that accounts for the right key performance indicators (KPIs). In other words, strategic foresight is a tool to run your business on a supercharged view of the future.

However, focusing on strategic foresight will involve breaking out of your comfort zone. Everyone loves to be an expert, but this process involves letting go of what you think you know and being prepared to delve into areas that you have little or no knowledge of yet. My role as a consultant and facilitator is to consistently push you out of your comfort zone so that you're always challenging and looking for a different space.

Traditional strategy consulting v strategic foresight

It can be helpful to compare traditional methods of strategy consulting with the strategic foresight journey to see how the world has changed, and how you and your organisation need to change to keep up with it.

Traditional strategy consulting	Strategic foresight journey
Facts	Strategic conversations into the uncertainty of unknown-unknowns
Research	Asking questions; scanning for signals and wildcards
Desktop analysis (numbers driven)	Go experience the future (empathy, get out of the building)
Bring in experts	Bring in ecosystem partners and stakeholders for the journey
Know which questions to ask	Don't know which questions to ask all the time

Strategic Copilot
A CEO's Guide to Changing Times

Traditional strategy consulting	Strategic foresight journey
Expect to know most of the answers	Expect to know few of the answers; emergent learning
Outside team does the job	Outside guide as expert facilitator; inside team does the work
3–12-month project	8–12 weeks for the initiation and plan phase, then continuous
Analyse the facts, make the recommendation	Explore the future, create understanding
Analyse best practice in the industry	Go visit and scan other organisations and businesses
Consultants own the tools, findings	Consultant-facilitator teaches the tools and method that the client owns, evolves the practice with them
Seek facts and clear answers	Happy with ambiguity
CEO presentation, recommendation	CEO coaching, executive support, guidance
Prefers one business model	Can handle several business model portfolios; explore-exploit

Another way to look at this is through two lenses: strategy as analysis and strategy as innovation.

Strategy as analysis		Strategy as innovation
Analytical, logical and linear	*Mindset*	Creative and disruptive
Logical	*Ambitions*	Offensive and transformational
Stable, expect it to be much like the present	*The future*	Unstable, expect it to be different
Rational actor	*People perspective*	Passion
Preserve and tune existing business model	*Business model*	Develop and test a portfolio of new business models
SWOT PESTEL Value-Chain Five-Forces	*Main tools*	Signal observation Strategic foresight/ Sense making Preferred scenario building Business model design Dynamic capabilities
Difficult, creates resistance	*Change*	Love to create it, make change happen

A CEO's Guide to Changing Times

Strategy as analysis		Strategy as innovation
Michael Porter, Big Consulting	*Leading proponent*	Gary Hamal, Rita McGrath

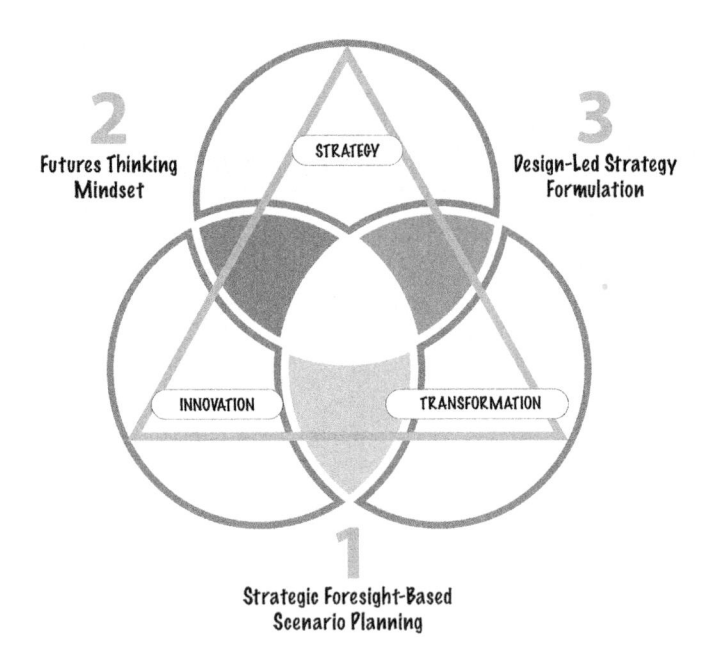

2 Futures Thinking Mindset

3 Design-Led Strategy Formulation

1 Strategic Foresight-Based Scenario Planning

STRATEGY

INNOVATION

TRANSFORMATION

Strategic Foresight chart

What feeds into strategic foresight?

There are several lines of questioning that we use to help our clients develop their strategic foresight. Answering each question that follows will provide you with different data that you can use to support future planning within your business. Before you ask yourself these questions, make sure you are clear on what your preferred version of the future looks like. The Five-Futures exercise I shared earlier in the book will be helpful here.

1. *How will we need to deliver customer value differently in our preferred future?* This will tell you how to organise your current structure, what skills and capabilities your people will need and whether your cultural values are going to change in your preferred future.

2. *How might innovation, R&D and product development look different in our preferred future?*

3. *How should we reframe our purpose for our preferred future?* Many of my clients found themselves asking this question following the Covid-19 pandemic because it was clear things had changed dramatically in a very short space of time.

4. *What key organisational processes may need to change?*

5. *How well does our current talent and workforce model serve us in different futures?*

6. *How might our current ways of working be challenged by the needs of our preferred scenarios and what types of digital platforms and systems may be required?* Many organisations went through a digital transformation as a result of the Covid-19 pandemic, for instance. Many have not fully returned to a pre-pandemic way of working after discovering how remote working could support the business and its people.

7. *How might our business model need to evolve as we pull it towards our preferred future?* This is where you would think about how it affects decision-making, culture and hiring into key roles.

8. *How do we empower our employees to do all of this and what data do we need?*

This is far from an exhaustive list of the questions you would ask while developing the strategic foresight at your organisation, but these questions are a good starting point. The purpose is to broaden your view of the data you have available to you and to understand that asking the right question at the right time gives you deeper insights.

As I've already explained, mapping out different future scenarios that you can pivot between is essential in modern business. The world is moving faster than it ever

Chapter 12: Strategic Foresight

has and there is far less clarity over what will happen six months, one year or two years from now. You also have to embrace emergent learning. This means accepting that you're not only going to be learning from inside out, but also outside in. The latter is crucial, because you need a lot more insight from the outside than you ever have to stay ahead of trends.

Due to the speed with which the world now moves, we need to adopt a new way of working to keep up. Leaders need to make sure they are always seeking out new information, before it is available in the mainstream. This is crucial, because by the time something becomes common knowledge, the chance to capitalise has gone to one of your competitors who knew about it earlier than you did.

In Chapter 6 I shared how Toyota had taken a leap of faith by focusing on the development of their hybrid model, the Prius, when the major American carmakers were focusing on designing and manufacturing vehicles with ever-bigger petrol and diesel engines. Toyota positioned themselves as a sustainable automaker long before most of the world had considered the concept. As a result, they are now a long way ahead of their main competitors in this field.

How to have strategic conversations with your Board

There are certain elements that you need in place to have constructive strategic conversations with your Board. However, the most important is an underlying level of trust that allows both you as the CEO and the Board members to share their thoughts and opinions openly and honestly.

You need to be able to say to the Board: "Let's start with a clean sheet and go into this with an open mind". Too many times, I've seen CEOs who are scared to tell their Board members they want to challenge the current business model, but keeping quiet about these ambitions serves no one. I often help the CEOs I coach to practise having this conversation with their Board.

I can understand a CEO's reticence – if the Board has been in place for many years and the business has performed well, then saying you want a change of direction can feel akin to saying: "Your baby's ugly". But the fact is that without that honest dialogue, the business is likely to struggle in the fast-paced and highly changeable world in which we now live.

An important element of these challenging conversations is the framing. As a CEO, you need to learn how to suggest looking at things differently. Often that will mean providing the Board members with the data and proof required so that they convince themselves a change of direction is necessary.

In Chapter 9, we heard from John Nicols, who talked about how he helped Codexis diversify their product development and move away from focusing solely on biofuels, to the company's benefit. It would have been easy for John to continue with the plan put in place by his predecessor, but he saw the signs that momentum was shifting away from biofuels.

He spoke to the Board about seeking out new opportunities and alternative business models that would allow the investment the company had made in biofuels over the last five to ten years to be redirected effectively. That conversation led to analysis, and working with myself and my consultants, to find the best way forward using strategic foresight. The outcome was to try to sell or put on ice the biofuels element of the business, and focus on enzyme development for biopharma instead, which has been hugely successful for Codexis.

> "When I started at Codexis, there was a clear risk that a major transformation was likely to be needed, so I took the job with eyes mostly wide open ... I could see a way through but it wasn't clear that we were going to be able to achieve it. Then I found people in the company who

could see a way through and who were actually excited that we were going to refocus back on the pharmaceutical market, which is where we started out as a company ten years prior.

Trust in the leader is fundamental, as is transparency. If people are scared of what the leader is thinking and doing, they're not going to be as open, supportive and collaborative with you through this problem."

Let go of expected outcomes

Earlier in this chapter I mentioned the concept of emergent learning. What that really means is not being attached to a particular outcome or exact future when you go into strategic discussions. This is why, as a consultant, I may not have all the "right" questions lined up to begin with, but through facilitating discussions between key team members and experts, the path forward emerges.

A great example of this came some time ago when I was leading an offsite with Toyota in California. The company was preparing to launch its brand Scion, which was aimed at the gen Y market (broadly, those born between 1981–96). We started the strategic planning session with a sense that we were going to explore the launch and implementation strategy for Toyota Scion in the USA.

What we ended up with was something completely different. Our strategy became to hire coaches who would work with salespeople at the 1,200 US dealerships to coach them on how to sell cars to younger generations – in this case gen Y. In doing so, this would allow the coaches to explain how Scion was different to the cars that had come before.

Often people go into strategic planning sessions convinced that they have the right business model. Toyota's Scion division had planned to launch these cars in much the same way they had launched many other models. But when we carried out a study of Apple stores and explored how gen Y make purchases, we quickly realised that the old car sales technique of haggling and trying to push a car at a lower price was obsolete for this generation. This led to an open discussion about how you could develop two selling models within dealerships.

What I've observed having facilitated many offsite sessions for businesses is that after day one, most of the people feel frustrated at being brought out of their comfort zone. They have gone into this session thinking they know the result, and I've come along and deconstructed it all.

This leaves people feeling as though they're worse off than when they started, which leads to frustration. But over the course of day two and into day three I see the coin drop as the people involved reach a state of nirvana because they suddenly have clarity over what they're going to do and why. By contrast, at the start of the offsite they only had bits of a strategy or business model, but not the whole picture.

Crucially, what allows them to come together as a team is me as an external facilitator – I am able to take the internal politics out of the discussion and in doing so I help everyone to come together to focus on the challenge in hand and have fun in the process.

Creative destruction

The courage to self-disrupt using strategic foresight demands more than predicting the future – it requires the courage to demolish existing paradigms to rebuild stronger, more adaptive businesses. My associate William Malek, a seasoned facilitator of strategic foresight who you met earlier in the book, shared a pivotal experience with Cisco executives that exemplifies this principle.

Drawing inspiration from McKinsey's exploration of "creative destruction", as articulated by Richard Foster and Sarah Kaplan, William understood that traditional management philosophies often anchor organisations to outdated assumptions. To thrive in volatile markets, companies must disrupt themselves before external forces dictate their obsolescence. Cisco's leadership was about to confront this reality.

In the wake of the dotcom bubble, Cisco was on a trajectory to dominate both the home and corporate router markets. Yet, as an emerging IT titan, the company faced an existential question: could it remain relevant as technology evolved? Recognising this challenge, Cisco sent several executives to the Stanford University Advanced Project Management program, where they encountered William. He was later tasked with facilitating a bold exploration into disruptive opportunities that could challenge Cisco's on-premises business model.

At the time, the concept of virtual data centres – what we now call the cloud – was just beginning to take shape. Cisco executives, alongside top IT experts from major consultancies, gathered for a week-long offsite retreat to envision the future. The exercise was not merely speculative; it was a methodical deep dive into emerging trends and technologies. This included amplifying the drama with the internal debates and resistance during the process. One startling revelation emerged: Amazon, among others, was requesting routers of unprecedented scale from Cisco. This unusual demand signalled a tectonic shift.

The team quickly realised that the cloud could upend their entire business model, shifting demand away from on-premises solutions towards hybrid corporate data centres.

This insight was a wake-up call. The decision Cisco faced was stark: stay the course and risk irrelevance, or pivot towards this nascent but transformative technology. Thanks to the openness and foresight of its leadership, Cisco chose the latter. Over the next few years, the company transitioned from a primary focus on on-premises solutions to serving businesses migrating to hybrid and cloud-based models. Today, Cisco is a cornerstone of the IT industry, providing the infrastructure that powers the internet itself. This transformation underscores a vital truth: without the willingness to self-disrupt, even the mightiest organisations risk being eclipsed.

The key takeaway is that for organisations to thrive in an uncertain, rapidly evolving market, strategic foresight must go beyond theoretical exercises. It requires cultivating a culture of courage – one that challenges assumptions, embraces uncertainty and prioritises transformation before disruption becomes inevitable. With AI and quantum computing in its early emergent stage as I write this, what risks are you ignoring that could render your business obsolete?

Seven steps for strategic foresight

There are generally seven steps we work through when we are helping an organisation develop its strategic foresight. The ones myself and my team use were developed by William Malek. These steps are:

Chapter 12: Strategic Foresight

1. **Framing:** Frame the current situation.

2. **Scanning:** This is where you explore signals, wildcards and drivers of change. This is when you'll start to identify weak and strong signals, as we discussed in Chapter 6.

3. **Futuring:** This is when you identify and empathise alternative futures with stakeholders and ecosystem partners. Once options begin to emerge, you might decide you want to play in this field. Because you view the business landscape as an ecosystem, you might identify a partner to support you here.

4. **Visioning:** At this stage you're identifying scenarios in your preferred future.

5. **Envisioning:** Now that you know what future you're working towards, you'll develop business models to test your outputs and assumptions with potential stakeholders.

6. **Defining capabilities:** Next you define the capabilities you need to partner with a specific company or stakeholder, and you start working on developing any capabilities you don't already have.

7. **Moving forward:** This is when you begin implementing a portfolio of initiatives into your preferred future.

The key to getting the most from this framework is to begin with discussion before data, which feeds into the idea that you are working as part of an ecosystem and are not a standalone entity that operates in isolation.

You also need to bring together teams of people with different skills to ensure you cover all the bases. You need a team who can carry out analysis, and you need another team who is creative and comfortable thinking outside of the box. You also need at least one person to be involved who has an intuition about what is happening in the world and who is keeping an eye on where markets are going.

One of my top tips, which I learnt from author Tom Peters, is to hang around with "crazy" people and listen to what they have to say. If you do, you'll come across some of the next big ideas long before they hit the mainstream and it's too late to capitalise.

You also need to think carefully about who is best placed to join these sessions around strategic foresight. Who you bring in will depend on what market you are trying to target, what support you have access to and can afford, and what kind of business you're in.

In some cases it will be appropriate to bring in staff that mimic buyer avatars, if your products target their generation, because the executive team and Board may be more mature and therefore not think in the same way as new customer groups. Ideally, you'll bring in people who are directly in touch with your customers, because they will be able to help you identify your preferred future and reframe your current strategy based on your customers. If you're branching out into a completely new area, you may want to involve a strategic partner who has more knowledge of this new marketplace than you.

Factors that allow strategic foresight to succeed

There are several factors that need to be in place to allow this process of developing strategic foresight to succeed.

1. **Executive team buy-in:** The executive team must buy into the strategic, emergent learning journey process. You and the rest of your team need to be open to not knowing all the answers, and to accept that this process of discovery will strengthen your position.

2. **Be engaged in the process:** All those involved need to be engaged in and motivated to be part of this process. You need to be open to apply new

capabilities in yourself. You have to be prepared to be part of a team or group that you may never have imagined joining. You might mess up. In some cases you might have to approach research and marketing in a different way.

3. **Create structure:** As you engage in a long-range preferred future, you need to have clearly defined strategic processes in place for managing your project portfolio and a structure to allow you to see how you're performing.

To access additional resources around the theme of taking the long view and developing strategic foresight, scan the following QR code:

Finding Support

As you will no doubt have gathered by this stage, developing strategic foresight and choosing a direction of travel in such an uncertain world is challenging, if not impossible to do alone. That is, if you want to do it well. Gone are the days when the CEO was expected to have all the answers. In the 21st century, the CEOs that lead the best performing organisations know that they don't have all the answers and they seek out support to help them find the answers.

They are not afraid to use the collective intelligence of their teams to help them uncover blind spots, develop strategies and make decisions under challenging circumstances. But even if you have an exceptional executive team, you still need an outside view to help you truly see all the options.

This outside view may come from a consultant like myself. It could come from a trusted friend, adviser or mentor who you have a long-standing relationship with. Alternatively, you may find that partnering with a stakeholder who is also part of your ecosystem brings great value. Or it may come from speaking to your customers and getting their perspectives. Often, it will involve a combination of these options.

Finding the right support can feel like a challenge. It is also not something you do just once. In fact, finding the right support relies on you having a strong external network of people whom you can trust.

Building Networks and Trusted Advisers

I believe that building networks, internal and external, is essential. From my perspective, the reason I particularly value external networks is because I always want to have options. I want to have a network of people who I can phone to find out information about different markets, industries or locations. This is where some of the greatest value lies in strong external networks.

We also live in an age where online misinformation is a genuine challenge. It is sometimes hard to discern fact from fiction and this is why a network of high-integrity people who you trust is so valuable. Your network should be made up of people who you trust can tell you what is real and what is not.

Strategic Copilot
A CEO's Guide to Changing Times

My personal motto, after years of introspection, is to have lifelong professional relationships. I want to have a good relationship with everyone I work with, whether I'm consulting for them or they are providing a service to me. As a result of taking this approach, I have built up a strong network of people I trust.

Internal v external networks

As I've mentioned, there are two different sides to building networks – internal and external. In my experience, a lot of CEOs and executives, particularly those who have been with their organisation for a while, tend to go to their internal team for support and information regarding sticky matters. Many fast-growing businesses rely on their internal teams around 95 per cent of the time when they're seeking information to help them untangle problems and make decisions.

However, in doing so they are neglecting valuable external sources of information. These are people who may have other insights into markets and other countries that you and your internal team don't. I'm not saying that you shouldn't use your internal team to support you, but you do have to differentiate between what facts and information you want to come from internal sources, and what facts and information you want to receive via your external networks.

Chapter 13:
Building Networks and Trusted Advisers

When you are seeking step-out growth, it's essential that your top team are people who are supportive of and willing to step out of your organisation's comfort zone and perhaps enter new markets. You need people around you who are not reluctant to change and seek new opportunities.

In my career, I have also seen a reluctance among some management teams to bring in external support. External consultants can be branded "a waste of money" rather than viewed through the lens of the value they can add, in part because of their external position.

Developing your internal network

Once you have established that you have the right people in your team, who are willing to step outside their comfort zone, you need to ensure that they are constantly developing and refreshing their knowledge. The longer someone stays in one company, the easier it is for them to become embedded in that culture and the current way of doing things.

One of the ways to counter this is to ensure your people are regularly attending conferences and events, particularly ones where they can interact with your customers. But as I've said already, often by the time you read about something online or in the news, it's too late. A lot of the breakthroughs in any industry happen on the periphery of what's known. This is why developing a strong external network to complement your internal network is essential.

There are ways to explore using internal members of your team more effectively, such as by having a strong business development team, or ensuring there are always people out and about at conferences and talking to your customers. However, there is a great deal of value in also using external consultants, not only to help you find opportunities you may otherwise miss, but also for the development of your internal teams.

Working with a consultant on a project puts the junior and senior members of the team on a similar footing and supports them to learn from each other, while working on a project to benefit the business.

In every business, the balance between internal and external sources of information will be different. This also varies between markets. For example, in the Middle East, businesses prefer to have employees and rely more heavily on their internal resources, whereas in the USA, there is a tendency to rely more on contractors or consultants, particularly in very fast-moving sectors.

Chapter 13:
Building Networks and Trusted Advisers

Going from external to internal

Fostering lifelong professional relationships can be highly beneficial for your business. Around half of the businesses I work with have been successful by bringing in people they trust who they have previously worked with. The people the executives and CEOs bring in are ones who they know can get results.

In a world where around 70 per cent of people lie on their CVs, knowing that someone can do what they promise is incredibly valuable.[34] This is also why I recommend checking any prospective employee's LinkedIn profile to see what kind of network they have and what those people say about them.

It's also important to recognise that in this day and age, people move between jobs much more frequently than they ever did before. Job cycles are getting shorter, so even if someone who you value within your business moves on, that may not mean they are gone forever. There is a good chance that if their skills and values align with the strategic direction your company takes, they will find their way back to you a little later in their career.

---

34   Robinson, B., PhD (2023) "70% of Workers Lie on Resumes, New Study Shows," Forbes, 7 November. Available at: https://www.forbes.com/sites/bryanrobinson/2023/11/05/70-of-workers-lie-on-resumes-new-study-shows/.

Bringing people in who can hit the ground running can make all the difference to the success of your business, especially at upper levels of management. I know of one client who brought someone from their external network into their business, and the new hire had found and initiated an acquisition within one month of starting work.

Understanding the need for external support

The world is moving faster now than it ever has. We inhabit a VUCA world, and the old style of planning where you looked three to five years ahead doesn't help you understand the capabilities you need or to adapt those capabilities in the face of so much change.

There is still a lot of negative stigma around consultants, partly because there is often a lack of understanding about what the return on investment will be, and because businesses don't budget enough. Not budgeting enough for consultancy services often makes the problem worse. It means the business is likely to end up with second-rate consulting help which may not go all the way to solving the issue. This only reinforces the belief that paying for consulting is a waste of money. This is why it's so important to find the right-fit consultant for your needs and your organisation.

Chapter 13:
Building Networks and Trusted Advisers

Earlier in the book I talked about the psychometric testing tools we use to help our clients understand where they may have gaps in their teams, in terms of both skills and knowledge. Filling those gaps becomes a lot easier when you have a strong external network.

This is also important when you are taking a long view of your strategy, because it's critical that you not only understand your team composition, but also that the people on your team understand what they are good at. If you want to innovate and move into new markets, myself and my team can often tell you very quickly where your gaps are simply by looking at your team composition. We can highlight the blind spots you might have, and in doing so ensure you have a stronger foundation for success.

Building your external network

There are many ways in which you can build an external network, but one of the most effective I have found is to join clubs. When I returned to live in the UK in 2017, I had been living out of the country for 27 years. I wanted to quickly build a network, and to find people I loved working with, so I joined a range of members' clubs and professional groups.

When you join a club, you're guaranteed to meet people who have a similar interest to you and the time it takes you to bond with others is accelerated when you have something in common. Also, if you join a club because of an interest or passion, even if you don't meet anyone for your professional network you will likely still have a good time.

The other thing I gain from being an active member of many clubs, and from having worked all over the world, is my multiperspectivity. I've developed this from talking to a lot of different people with different personalities and learning from all of them. One of the best lessons to learn is that even if you don't agree with someone, you can still learn from them.

> **The six thinking hats technique**
>
> If you are trying to develop this multiperspectivity then the techniques from *Six Thinking Hats* by Edward de Bono[35] are just as valuable today as they were when I first started using them over 30 years ago. Each of the six people in the room gets a different coloured hat, and each hat is associated with a different perspective on the problem at hand. The group then discusses this problem, but each individual is only allowed to speak on it from the perspective that aligns with their hat.

---

35   De Bono, E. (1985) *Six Thinking Hats*. Little, Brown and Company.

Chapter 13:
Building Networks and Trusted Advisers

> This means you get a range of views around the table – some negative, some positive and some neutral – and in doing so you explore the issue from all angles.

Working with a strategy copilot

I act as a strategy copilot for many of my clients, which is a different role to that of a coach or a mentor. As a copilot my role is to be a sounding board for my clients and to help them arrive at a decision. Another way to imagine this relationship is that I am the navigator, while you – the CEO or executive – are the one with their hands on the controls.

As a copilot, I help leaders to see all the possible routes available to them, and I help them choose the most suitable for their business and their broader goals. It's important that I'm an external voice in this process. Internally, especially in larger corporate organisations, people have their own agendas and interests in what are typically complex businesses.

I differ in that I'm an external figure. I have no preference other than to help you arrive at the right decision for your company to achieve success. Because I am outside the company, I can also create a sacred space where a CEO can talk through issues that they may not be comfortable discussing with their team. This allows you to have an open discussion and critically examine every aspect of a decision before you decide what path to take. In many cases, decisions involve making a tradeoff, and my role as copilot is to bring a multitude of perspectives to the table to help you find the right tradeoff in any given situation.

I have interviewed many successful leaders in the years that I have been writing my blog and recording my podcast, and one theme that comes up repeatedly is the boost they receive from having an outside perspective when they are making decisions and discussing business strategy.

When I'm in the role of strategy copilot, I can bring a stabilising force and smooth the "landing" of any decision. I do this by helping the CEO talk through all the possibilities and prepare for different responses or scenarios. I'm helping them to navigate change that can drive business transformation.

To accept this level of outside help, you need to be humble, curious and you need to overcome your ego. Too many CEOs and executives still see seeking external help as a sign of weakness, when the reality is that in the fast-paced world we live in, not seeking external help will become a true weakness and lead to missed opportunities for the business.

Chapter 13:
Building Networks and Trusted Advisers

Jon Rawding, who you met earlier in the book, talks about the value an external adviser can bring in his own book *Learning Beyond Limits*. His key takeaway on the topic of external support is:

> "An external adviser can add significant value to not only your development as a leader, but also to the development of the company you work for. I can't stress enough the value of having an impartial external perspective, and someone you can talk to who challenges you in all the right ways.
>
> Building a strong relationship with an external adviser will take time, but it is worth the investment. The key is to find someone who complements your strengths and who works differently to you, because that will help broaden your perspective and highlight new opportunities."[36]

To access additional resources around the theme of finding support as a CEO, scan the following QR code:

---

36   Rawding, J. (2024) *Learning Beyond Limits: Leadership Lessons from Life's Journey*. Independently published.

Strategic Copilot
A CEO's Guide to Changing Times

Business Technology & Innovation

If everything in the world is changing, it stands to reason that businesses need to change if they are to survive. Innovation is a form of positive change. It's a way to take the signals you see around you and turn it into a new product or service that can benefit your existing customers, or allow you to expand into a new niche.

As you and I well know, organisations can't afford to stand still. Innovation is the lifeblood of any long-lasting, sustainable business. Doing what you've always done might seem tempting, but at some point the world will move on. When this happens, you will struggle to catch up to your competitors.

Strategic Copilot
A CEO's Guide to Changing Times

In the 21st century, the world is moving on more rapidly. Cycles of change are getting shorter. There is a great deal of uncertainty in the world as I write this, and while uncertainty can feel destabilising, it is also the perfect breeding ground for innovation. The key is to use your executive mindset to embrace uncertainty and find the opportunities that lie within it.

Chapter 14

Uncertainty – Obstacles to Innovation

Uncertainty can be experienced from many different perspectives, and a key to future innovation may be understanding the nuances through which people and organisational cultures experience uncertainty as a present, evolving and moving situation.

I talked earlier in the book about the uncertainty we face from external sources, so what we're going to examine here is uncertainty from an internal perspective and how we can define innovation as a psychic opposite of uncertainty that focuses on confidence, creativity and leadership.

Uncertainty is an internal state of mind, within you as CEO or your leadership team, and it manifests in different ways. The first type of uncertainty tends to stop forward motion by creating a circular backward motion of second-guessing around issues, process, security, health and safety. Leadership teams that fall into this type of uncertainty tend not to make any decisions because they don't feel they know enough.

This leads into the second type of uncertainty that takes the form of complacency. This manifests as an unwillingness to disrupt or take risks because you have it easy and things are working. In other words, a business' leadership team chooses to continue doing the same thing rather than building on success by doing something different.

Pre-Covid, there were many companies that could have moved forwards very fast, but the pandemic disrupted their operations to the point that they either lost a great deal of money or went under altogether. This was because they had been relying on being able to do what they always had. When the world changed, they were unable to adapt quickly enough to keep up.

Innovation as a state of mind arises from confidence. It comes from a belief in yourself and your team that you can evaluate the current situation and come to meaningful conclusions. Much of what I've already

Chapter 14:
Uncertainty – Obstacles to Innovation

discussed throughout this book feeds into this mindset. It is also closely connected to the intrapreneurial spirit, which is all about seeing an unmet need with crystal clarity and being willing to invent new solutions and take new directions to meet that need, even if it goes against some of the fabric of the existing organisation.

There are many great examples of innovation that occur through combining existing elements into a radical new product, service or business solution. An example of this form of innovation comes from General Electric. They built the business selling glass for aeroplane cockpits, but about 20 years ago they also moved into financing their product. This meant people could lease the cockpit glass rather than buying it outright.

Forms of uncertainty

Within business, there are four forms of uncertainty that you are most likely to encounter:

1. **Crumbling foundations:** This is when the foundations on which you have built your business shift before your eyes. An example is the new regulation introduced for UK businesses post-Brexit, where many saw their existing ways of operating disappearing before their eyes.

2. **Conflicting signs on the road ahead:** In this kind of uncertainty, you aren't sure which way a situation is going to play out. For example, when Russia invaded Ukraine, some people felt the conflict would only last a few months, and made their future plans based on this. As we now know, this conflict has lasted far longer and affected far more of the world economy than many initially predicted.

3. **Speed of change:** When things are moving very fast, you are forced to make a series of decisions quickly because you are going through multiple cycles of change. In this situation, you can feel as though you are in a high-speed tunnel that you can't see out of. Things don't seem clear, you become tired of making decisions that involve a gamble and decisions end up being made without rational thought.

4. **Multiple street signs leading to overwhelm:** This is when there is so much changing around you and so much new information to absorb that you become confused, perplexed and have a complete meltdown. A good example of this was when social media first emerged. There were plenty of people who thought it was a phase. There were many others who banked entire businesses on it. Then there were many who found it hard to work out

Chapter 14:
Uncertainty – Obstacles to Innovation

which of the many emerging platforms to target. Those who took decisive action came out ahead, while those who became paralysed by choice struggled to make meaningful headway.

As a CEO, the key to surviving in our increasingly volatile and fast-changing world is to learn how to take these different forms of uncertainty and see them as opportunities for innovation, rather than something overwhelming.

You have to be able to future forecast in a way that focuses on effectiveness rather than accuracy. Take a weather forecast as an example. An accurate weather forecast might say, "Tomorrow is going to be very hot at 35 degrees C", but an effective forecast would say, "Tomorrow the weather is going to be in the mid-30s so dress in light, cool clothes". The point is, you don't necessarily need to know the precise temperature to make a decision about what you might wear or what you might do the following day.

How to transform uncertainty into innovation

One of the ways in which you can turn uncertainty into innovation is to use the demolition and reconstruction strategy I discussed in Chapter 12. It's important that you have external support for these demolition exercises to help you avoid the trap of groupthink,[37] and to ensure that everyone on your executive team is listened to. It's also important to note that these demolition sessions might result in your strategy staying the same.

In this scenario, the difference will be in the alignment of the executive team. When you deconstruct and then reconstruct your strategy together, you confirm that it's solid and everyone feels as though they have played their part in creating it.

Communication within your executive team is a crucial component for transforming uncertainty into innovation, but so too is communicating bad news and delivering feedback. Some people don't take feedback well, even when it is intended to help them. This often stems from their previous experiences triggering them when they receive feedback.

You can't wait until someone has a tantrum and throws their toys out of the pram before you deal with an issue – when something like this has happened, it's too late. What we recommend to keep communication within your executive team where it needs to be is to continually

---

[37] "Groupthink" is a term coined by social psychologist Irving Janis in his 1972 book *Victims of Groupthink: A Psychological Study of Foreign-Policy Decisions* and Fiascoes, and refers to the tendency of groups to prioritise consensus over critical thinking and diverse perspectives.

Chapter 14:
Uncertainty – Obstacles to Innovation

work through Tuckman's stages of team development: forming, storming, norming, performing.[38]

The stages of team development

In case you're not familiar with Tuckman's model, I've set out each of the stages here, as it's a useful way to better understand team behaviours and how to manage them to increase productivity and improve your processes.

1. Forming

In the forming stage, team members come together, often tentatively, as they establish roles, responsibilities and shared goals. When a new team forms, there's typically a sense of excitement mixed with uncertainty.

As the leader, your role is to encourage open dialogue to allow the team to clarify their expectations, roles and objectives. At this stage it's crucial to set a foundation for trust by promoting transparency and listening to each member of the team.

---

38   MIT Human Resources (no date) "Using the stages of team development". Available at: https://hr.mit.edu/learning-topics/teams/articles/stages-development.

You need to provide clear direction, establish the team's purpose early on and create a psychologically safe environment where everyone feels able to share their opinions and feels valued.

2. Storming

Differences in working styles, priorities or opinions tend to surface during this stage, leading to conflicts and power struggles. This stage can be uncomfortable, especially when team members express frustration and anger about a perceived lack of progress. But going through storming is essential for the team to grow.

The key to reaching the growth phase following storming is to actively manage conflict. You can do this by encouraging healthy debates and stressing the need for everyone to behave respectfully. To pass through the storming phase and have a stronger team on the other side, you need to resolve any disagreements constructively.

It is essential to address any issues you identify early. If you don't, they will escalate and become much larger problems within the team. It is helpful to refocus discussions around the team's goals to ensure everyone is aligned. Emphasise the need for a collaborative approach and having open discussions.

Chapter 14:
Uncertainty – Obstacles to Innovation

3. Norming

As you move into the norming stage, the team begins to resolve conflicts, develop trust and establish norms for how to work together. Roles and processes become clearer, while team members feel comfortable sharing and receiving constructive criticism.

Your role is to make sure that every member of the team feels heard and appreciated. Make sure you reinforce positive behaviours and establish a regular pattern of communication. This might involve regular team meetings alongside individual check-ins. The aim through these meetings is to keep everyone on the team aligned and focused on the bigger goal.

The more you can encourage the members of your team to bond, the more you'll see a shared sense of accountability evolve. As the team collaborates more effectively, performance improves and you will start to see meaningful progress being made towards the team's shared goals.

4. Performing

This is when the team reaches a high level of efficiency and effectiveness. During this stage, team members work seamlessly towards shared objectives. Collaboration is fluid, and trust is strong.

One of the hallmarks of this stage of the model is that team members may switch roles to support the best outcomes for the team. They will appreciate each other's differences and know how these contribute to the team's overall success.

To maintain the performing stage, you need to focus on creating a culture of continuous improvement, which is underpinned by encouraging feedback and adapting processes if and when required. To maintain motivation, celebrate the team's successes.

For a team to become high-performing, and stay there, they need to be empowered to make their own decisions and take ownership of their work. As a leader, that means you focus less on the day-to-day management and instead turn your attention to the team's strategic goals to help everyone stay on track.

Although Tuckman's model is presented as linear, the truth is that teams rarely progress through these stages in a linear fashion. Changes, such as new team members joining, organisational shifts or external challenges, can cause a team to regress to earlier stages (e.g. back to storming). The trick is in knowing which stage your team is in, and what you need to do to either move them on to the next stage, or help them stay in the "performing" stage as long as possible. When you can do this, you

Chapter 14:
Uncertainty – Obstacles to Innovation

are more likely to maintain stability and productivity within your team.

Applying Tuckman's model to executive teams

Executive teams often face unique pressures, such as high-stakes decision-making and diverse opinions among strong leaders. Regularly revisiting Tuckman's model ensures that the channels of communication remain open and are productive, and that conflicts are addressed before they sour and become toxic for all involved.

By working through this model, you will consistently reinforce trust and collaboration, which are the foundations for high performance. Your aim should always be to maintain a culture of mutual respect and high performance. Tuckman's model provides a useful shared language and understanding that can help you manage the dynamics of your executive team in a productive way.

The value of keeping your customers close

The world is no longer two-dimensional. There are many perspectives and shifting layers to the picture we see in front of us that need to be accounted for. Often things are moving so fast that you need to address them in real time. There isn't time to carry out pilots and have multiple meetings over many months to make a decision.

To understand potential problems and opportunities, you need to simulate them with your team, so that should they arise, you already have an idea of how to respond. One of the most important aspects of this work is becoming aligned and reaching conclusions together as a team.

Having a flatter organisational hierarchy is hugely beneficial when you are carrying out this kind of multiperspective thinking in a group, because it means you really do understand your customers and what they're thinking. Ideally, you have zero distance from your customer, which means you understand them and their challenges as intimately as if they were your own.

Terry Fisher, who I introduced you to earlier, struggled to get Thomas Cook's Board to move in the right direction when he was CEO precisely because they were too far removed from their customers. The Board couldn't recognise how the travel industry had changed following the dotcom boom. So, when Terry was recommending selling their planes and hotels, and instead moving to become an online travel agency, the Board dug in.

> "The problem I had was that the Board didn't share the vision that I had for the business. They believed that they had such a strong brand and

Chapter 14:
Uncertainty – Obstacles to Innovation

such a strong name that they didn't need to evolve to become an online player. They were also incredibly asset led – they owned aeroplanes and hotels – but there was really no reason in those days for Thomas Cook to run an airline. There were plenty of low-cost airline carriers where we could have bought seats much more cheaply and become asset-less.

We could have put hundreds of millions of dollars into the bank. We could have sold the aeroplanes and hotels, and we could have invested that into online technology. But the Board didn't see it. They didn't like my strategy. I was CEO of a business that I thought was going to fail, so I resigned because I wanted to try and buy the business."

Terry's attempt to buy the business didn't work, and even though the Board did eventually come around to the strategy he had recommended, it was too late. For a short period, things began to look up for the travel agent, but in 2019 the business collapsed.

This demonstrates the importance of working to get everyone on the leadership teams and Board aligned around a strategy, because without that alignment, companies move too slowly. They try to ride out the uncertainty and often that leads to failure.

Embrace multiperspective thinking

To truly embrace multiperspective thinking, you need to have the right people around the table. In many cases that means bringing in outside experts, strategic thinkers and strategic specialists like myself. You need everyone on your executive team to buy into the idea of demolishing and reconstructing your strategy regularly. To do that effectively you need to communicate well.

Much earlier in my career, communication was considered a "soft skill" and often optional, which meant when a business ran out of money it killed its "soft skill" training. But with black swans floating down every corporate river in every country, and nothing guaranteed, businesses have woken up to the fact that there's nothing soft about communication. It's a hard, essential skill for your leadership team to have if they want the business to survive in the world as it is today.

There are many amazing leaders in the world as I write this, but too many underestimate the work they need to do continuously to bring up the leadership team below them. If you want to establish a company that is sustainable for the next 20–30 years, you need to focus on bringing in the right people at every level. You also need to focus on training the people several levels below

Chapter 14:
Uncertainty – Obstacles to Innovation

the executive team so that you have leaders who are ready to step up in the future.

When you can understand uncertainties, and the tools you can use to help you understand what is going on in our VUCA world, you will begin to see opportunities popping up all around you. By taking the time to assess the whole landscape, you can spot opportunities for innovation that will put you ahead of your competition.

Strategic Copilot
A CEO's Guide to Changing Times

AI and the Digital Transformation

As I write this, AI is the technology that everyone is talking about. Use of AI tools has exploded since OpenAI released ChatGPT in 2022 and there are more and more use cases emerging. Before we can talk constructively about AI and digital transformation, it is useful to first define what AI is at its core.

Peter Morgan, CEO of Deep Learning Partnership, described it as, "the technology that enables computers and machines to simulate human learning, reasoning, problem solving, decision making, creativity and autonomy" when he spoke at my Haig Talks event in

September 2024.[39] But Peter also pointed out that while this is the goal that many in the AI space are working towards, the technology is not at that level, yet.

Computing power, and therefore the power of AI, is increasing exponentially as I write this. In fact, some experts are predicting that we'll have achieved general artificial intelligence (AGI), which is a machine that is "conscious", by 2029. This simply demonstrates the rate at which this technology is developing.

But what does this mean for you, as a CEO, and your business? When we create an AGI, we will be able to use it for any business task you can think of. With that future seemingly not too far off, it's important to start asking yourself where you can use AI within your organisation, if you don't already. What business processes could you automate or streamline with AI?

Of course, there are concerns about what this means for workers, particularly those in low-skilled jobs who are most likely to be replaced by this technology, and least likely to have the ability to retrain. This is just one of the challenges you will have to manage as you lead your organisation through the fourth industrial revolution.

---

39   Haig Barrett Partners (2024) *Haig Talks - AI: Where are we headed?* Available at: https://www.youtube.com/watch?v=Ze3GsPZ5Z20.

Chapter 15:
AI and the Digital Transformation

The main point, however, is that you cannot afford to ignore AI or make the mistake of thinking that it isn't relevant in your industry or for your organisation. It is becoming relevant, and change is happening quickly.

Taking an AI-first approach

An AI-first approach to leadership means that you think proactively about how AI could be used in your business and what kind of people you need to employ to make the most of this technology. You need to think about all the elements within your business and what is going to change within each element as a result of the rise of AI.

This technology is changing so quickly that you can't afford to "wait and see". You need to be aware of it, do your best to understand it and find ways to use it in your organisation. If you don't, you risk being left behind.

When Paul Vatistas, Board Director and Senior Consultant at Haig Barrett Partners, spoke at the Haig Talks event I hosted in September 2024, he focused on what leaders need to do if they are to navigate this aspect of the digital transformation successfully.

To move beyond leadership and become a change agent, Paul explained leaders need to embrace an AI-first mindset.

"Leaders need to start thinking very differently about what they're doing. There is going to be a lot of change for people culture and there will be impacts on shared values as well.

The AI-first mentality is about learning, so if you're not spending part of every day trying to figure out what's happening today that was different from yesterday then you're going to get behind very, very quickly, and by 2029 that could be fatal [for your business].

Every job is going to change, not so much that they disappear, but the tasks within some of them are going to disappear and be replaced by AI agents completely in some cases and partially in others.

The challenge for leaders will be how do you retain and reprioritise your core values throughout this change? We're still human beings and we work with human beings. As leaders, we need to have good cultural values and reprioritise them to work in an AI-first world."[40]

---

40 Haig Barrett Partners (2024) *Haig Talks – AI: Where are we headed?* Available at: https://www.youtube.com/watch?v=Ze3GsPZ5Z20.

Chapter 15:
AI and the Digital Transformation

So, an AI-first approach doesn't mean you're going to replace all of your human employees with androids and robots. When you have an AI-first mentality, you have an open mind to how AI can support your business, whether that's in relation to your workflows, processes or products. During the innovation stages of product development, you will always have AI in mind in terms of what advantages it could bring.

Reserving a table at a restaurant is one example of where AI is making things easier for businesses and improving customer satisfaction. An AI chatbot that can answer the phone, take bookings and answer customer questions doesn't only mean that customers can complete bookings more quickly. It also means that restaurant staff aren't compromising on serving customers because they have to answer the phone to take bookings during busy periods.

The challenge for CEOs and other business leaders when it comes to adopting AI more widely within their organisations is breaking down the fear they feel about its potential complexity.

It's about people, not technology

Two men are walking in the forest. It's a sunny day and they've taken their shoes off to cool their feet in a nearby stream. As they're returning to the trail, they spot a bear in the distance. One man grabs his trainers, pulls them on and starts lacing them tightly. His friend watches him in disbelief.

"You're not going to be able to outrun a bear!" he says, incredulous.

The man pulling on his trainers looks up at him. "I don't have to outrun the bear, I just have to outrun you!" he shouts as he finishes lacing his shoes and takes off down the path ...

This is what having an AI-first mentality is all about. It's not about the technology. It's about outrunning your competitors. In a competitive world, I don't have to help my clients go as fast as possible, I have to help them go faster than their competitors. Even moving ten per cent faster than your nearest competitor will give you a significant advantage.

Imagine an oil services company is able to increase the speed with which it carries out one of its security processes by using AI. This also avoids a time stoppage in its operations, which therefore means it will get ahead of the competition.

What about using AI to analyse your supply chain transport routes? If this technology can plan ahead and find the optimum route for your drivers based on

Chapter 15:
AI and the Digital Transformation

conditions on the road each day it will save you time and make your operations more efficient.

The point is, you don't have to outrun the bear, you just have to outrun the guy behind you.

How do you outrun your competition when it comes to AI adoption? Getting ahead in this race has less to do with the technology itself and more to do with the collective intelligence of your team. The world is moving fast and in many different directions. New innovations are appearing all the time.

You need to leverage the collective intelligence of your executive team to help you find the best way forward, because there are too many variables and too many decisions required for any person on their own.

The other reason you need to leverage your team is that, as the CEO, you are not as close to your customers as you need to be. There will be signals in the marketplace and from your customers that you won't see. So, bring in your team. Talk to them. Communicate regularly about what you are all seeing and use that collective intelligence to make more robust business decisions.

Getting ahead in the race, whether with AI or other new technology, requires a collective performance. Your role in creating a strategy along with the rest of the executive team will only take your business so far. You need to roll that strategy out and ensure that your teams at every level understand and implement it.

These AI tools are available to everyone. What differentiates one business from another, more often than not, is not the tools they introduce but the way in which they train their people to use those tools. If you can do this better than your competitors, you will go to the front of the pack.

AI-driven efficiencies

I work a lot with engineering companies and those in the oil and gas industry. One area where I've seen AI tools used to great effect is digitising the service manuals for all manner of complex hydraulic equipment. This equipment will often need to be fixed in the field under challenging conditions.

In the past, those manuals were physical books, which engineers needed to refer to constantly. Some engineers with a great deal of experience would need the manual less frequently than their younger or less experienced counterparts. AI has levelled the playing field.

There are now AI tools that can identify what part you are looking at and automatically show you the relevant

Chapter 15:
AI and the Digital Transformation

part of the manual on your device. Some of these tools are even connected to the parts inventory, and can automatically order the parts your engineers will need to repair the equipment.

A company that adopts this technology will be more efficient and more versatile. Younger members of the team will have access to a depth of knowledge beyond their experience, allowing them to work more efficiently and shortening the learning curve in their roles. An AI tool could also flag potential mistakes, ensuring that fewer mistakes happen on the job. It will also gather data about which parts are failing most frequently, which will be valuable for future business and maintenance planning.

A survey conducted by *Forbes* in early 2023 found that over two-thirds (64 per cent) of business owners expect the use of AI to improve customer relationships and increase productivity within their businesses. The business owners questioned also stated that they believe AI will be an asset for improving decision-making, decreasing response times and avoiding mistakes.[41]

As I write this, we are still finding our way with AI implementation. However, this survey makes it clear

---

41   Haan, K. (2023) "How businesses are using artificial intelligence in 2024," *Forbes*. Available at: https://www.forbes.com/advisor/business/software/ai-in-business/.

that many believe in the tangible benefits AI can bring to organisations. Therefore, any CEOs that resist its use will likely see their businesses start to lag behind competitors who leverage this evolving technology to their advantage.

To access additional resources around the theme of business technology and innovation, scan the following QR code:

A New Approach to Work

Although the way in which we work was evolving prior to 2020, the pace of change was nothing compared to what we all experienced during the Covid-19 pandemic. Overnight, people went from going to offices to working from their homes. Suddenly, the connectivity of our modern world provided a lifeline not only for individuals, but for businesses, in the face of an unprecedented event.

But home working and having greater flexibility around how we fit our jobs into our lives is not the only way in which our approach to work has changed. Businesses are increasingly recognising the value of allowing their employees greater freedom within their roles to allow them to focus on their passions.

While this isn't always possible, the companies that find a way to support "intrapreneurs" are able to keep key talent and innovate to outgrow their competitors. Younger generations who are entering the workforce increasingly want roles with a sense of purpose. They aren't just coming to work for a pay cheque. An organisation that can provide that sense of purpose to its employees has a significant opportunity for step-out growth.

When your people are fully engaged in your overall mission, they will give greater discretionary effort and will actively seek improvements for the business. In this day and age, the value of employee engagement cannot be underestimated.

The Rise of the Intrapreneur

An intrapreneur is anyone inside a corporate organisation who is there to innovate in some way, whether that's to change the business model, or come up with new products or services. In the last 20–25 years, many large organisations have explored how they can become more entrepreneurial.

The start of this trend was the tech boom of the late 1990s and early 2000s, when many large companies started losing talent to startups which allowed for more freedom, innovation and creativity. Many big businesses realised that they needed to retain this talent and this was when the concept of the intrapreneur was born.

Intrapreneurs are typically given more freedom to develop their own cultures within the divisions they set up and run at a larger organisation. Their role is to develop an innovative project or idea that will enhance the company's future. The key is that people working in corporate jobs who have an entrepreneurial spirit now have an outlet for their entrepreneurial talent. This makes them more fulfilled at work and benefits the business too.

Generally, intrapreneurs are also given autonomy to work on their projects, because those in executive leadership positions recognise that often these kinds of ventures can have a considerable positive impact on the company. This impact is not only felt in monetary terms but also in relation to a company's strategy and direction.

Intrapreneurs tend to be highly motivated individuals who not only have a specific skill set and leadership capabilities, but who also have an innovative vision that others within the corporation can get behind. Encouraging a culture of intrapreneurship is an excellent way to allow a larger business to innovate more quickly and efficiently.

The rise of the intrapreneur

As I mentioned, intrapreneurship began to become a much greater focus for corporations around the time of the dotcom boom, not only because startups were

Chapter 16:
The Rise of the Intrapreneur

attracting a great deal of talent, but because the launch of the internet suddenly made the world much more accessible.

Prior to the internet, innovation was largely restricted to big companies that had the funds to support R&D, and to then develop products and services as a result of that R&D.

Voice-over-IP calling meant that it was no longer prohibitively expensive to conduct business calls with people overseas. The likes of Google made digital file sharing not only possible, but also affordable. Video calling software, like Zoom, now means it's possible to have video conferences with dozens of participants all over the world for minimal cost. Even 30 years ago, hosting a video conference required expensive and onerous video conferencing systems that were fixed in place in an office.

We are increasingly seeing startups being bought out by larger companies. Corporations are happy to buy these kinds of businesses that have stemmed from someone, or a small group of people, with an intense passion for a project. The truth is that innovation is easier with smaller teams who have fewer rules and processes to follow.

A good example of where big business was damaged by the rise of startups and intrapreneurs is the contrast between Japan and the USA in the early 2000s. Japanese corporations, and particularly Sony, dominated the music market at this time. That is, until the iPod came along. What this demonstrated was that culturally Japanese businesses fell behind.

In Japan, following processes and rules was much more culturally important than it was in the USA. As a result, many businesses started up in people's garages in LA and elsewhere in California, and then went on to become world-leading corporations. Meanwhile the big Japanese companies like Sony that should have retained their leadership role in the music industry found themselves struggling to keep up with the innovation coming out of the nimble startups in the USA.

Following the significant loss in market share for many Japanese tech businesses with the rise of Apple and other US-based corporations, the Japanese government encouraged companies that all focused on the same product sector to consolidate. The thinking was that having just one or two businesses in areas like TVs, music players and so on, would allow them to operate closer to the bleeding edge of the tech where they could move faster, invest more money and see opportunities coming earlier.

Chapter 16:
The Rise of the Intrapreneur

How to invest in intrapreneurship

Large corporations need to financially invest in intrapreneurship. They also need to help people develop an innovation mindset, as well as providing people with the autonomy to innovate and create. In terms of financial investment, one of the tools I would recommend using is zero budgeting – although I am aware many executive teams shy away from this because of the work and time it takes them in review.

However, the concept of zero budgeting is one that many Fortune 100 chief financial officers (CFOs) would love to use. The way it works is simple. Every year, each division starts with a budget of zero and they have to justify any money they want the company to spend in their area. The advantage of this is that it makes it much easier to financially allocate 20–30 per cent of your R&D budget to new ventures that could catapult you ahead of your competition.

The downside is that reviewing the applications for each division's budget takes time. In many corporations that already have an R&D structure of hundreds of people, the task seems too onerous. Therefore, instead they broadly repeat the same budget in each division based on what they received the previous year.

An alternative approach to zero budgeting is to explore partnership and joint venture (JV) opportunities. This is when it is helpful to think of the market in which you operate as an ecosystem. Doing so encourages you to look for smaller organisations that are innovating in your space and partner with them, or establish a JV, to help you innovate without restructuring your current R&D team.

When you are seeking potential partners, look to adjacent markets as well as those in which you already operate. You may be able to establish joint development agreements with minimal financial outlay at the outset. If you find a smaller company doing something really interesting, you may decide to go down the route of an acquisition. These are all options open to you and should form part of the discussion about your broader strategic picture.

You may also decide you want to develop more intrapreneurs within your company. One organisation I would recommend to help develop people with intrapreneurial tendencies is Innov8rs. You might be surprised by how many different ways you can out-innovate your competition once you start to dabble in intrapreneurship.

Chapter 16:
The Rise of the Intrapreneur

Case study: Home Grown

Earlier in the book you met Andrew Richardson, who is Managing Director of Home House. He spoke with me about the creation of the Home Grown brand, which has helped the business expand significantly.

Andrew explained that at the time Home Grown started, the company's then-CEO asked him to pitch for creating a new club on the doorstep of one of Home House's existing properties. It took him some time to see the opportunity, but once he did he ran with the idea.

> "I knew I needed to find a point of difference for this club. It was in a residential area, so there was no chance of any late-night noise or a nightclub-type scenario. Then I looked around Home House, and of course a lot of people have their own organisations or businesses. There is a lot of investment in startups and scale-ups and a lot of meetings taking place, but Home House was always about getting people together socially.
>
> Then the idea came to have a community that is aimed at supporting entrepreneurs on their growth journeys. I spoke to a few people who had invested in entrepreneurs, and I attended a

> few seminars about the entrepreneur's journey, and that's how the idea was born."
>
> Andrew's pitch was accepted and the Home Grown branch of Home House was born. Based in London, the Home Grown club has a community of 1,500 professionals and has attracted a range of high-profile ambassadors. It has also won a range of awards and has plenty of success stories to share from its members.

Self-organising, autonomous teams

A concept that William Malek shared with me when we spoke on *The Board Perspective*, is that of self-organising, autonomous teams.[42] These teams are not told what to do, instead they are developing their own strategies. It's the premise that Chinese company Haier is using to great effect.

> "Those strategies inform this kind of living organisation and living system, allowing the system to grow. But [the teams] are highly accountable for producing value and they're

---

42 Haig Barrett Partners (2021) *Why Transform – The Board Perspective: Episode 1 with William Malek*. Available at: https://www.youtube.com/watch?v=W1-XCvv1nHQ.

Chapter 16:
The Rise of the Intrapreneur

reporting to the customer. You'll often hear Chairman John tell his people: 'You don't report to me. You don't report to a boss. Your boss is your customer and you must fundamentally make that mindset shift.' This is, to a large degree, the mindset that is at the core for highly successful entrepreneurs."

William goes on to describe how the system in place at Haier is designed to "unleash the innate human potential of the people who come into the organisation". By placing the focus on the customer, those working for the organisation can take greater responsibility for their work and feel a greater sense of purpose.

Develop a "fixer" mindset

The TV show *Ray Donovan* is a fictional series about a professional "fixer" to the rich and famous in Hollywood. While I wouldn't recommend that you emulate Ray Donovan's extreme actions, what I do suggest is exploring how to bring together the logical and the creative, which is the defining trait of this kind of mindset.

During the Covid-19 pandemic, the companies that adopted a fixer mindset were the ones that got ahead and solved problems more quickly and more innovatively than others. This is an extension of the entrepreneurial and intrapreneurial mindset, where you are looking to do things quicker, cheaper and better.

There are different levels to the fixer mindset, and different businesses will need to access these different levels at different times.

- **Being fast-paced with lots of chopping and changing. You can't let yourself get in the way:** This relates to the culture you create in your organisation. Having autonomous teams that are given the freedom to innovate is important – like in the Haier example from Chapter 5. You also have to be adaptable at an organisational, as well as at a team, level. As a CEO, you need the right team to support you, so it is in your interest to bring in people who are creative and intrapreneurial to lead in this area.

    As I explained in Chapter 9, you need to create processes that provide the necessary guardrails without completely removing or overly restricting creativity and autonomy.

- **Not being emotionally attached to a solution. You need to negotiate difficult decisions, always have the stakeholder in mind and leave your ego behind:** I once worked with someone in a big corporation who engineered

Chapter 16:
The Rise of the Intrapreneur

themselves out of a job, because it was the right thing to do. This is the epitome of not being emotionally attached to a solution. In short, the organisation needed to become flatter. His job was one that went in this new flatter hierarchy. I take my hat off to him for making that decision, because many people wouldn't have been so pragmatic in his situation. Organisations in general need to become flatter to survive in this fast-paced world, because everything moves so quickly that there isn't time for decisions to go up and down the chain of command.

The main thing, in any situation, is to think through all the options and not block any off before you've fully explored them. This is why having someone to act as a sounding board is so important. Often, having that sounding board be someone external like a strategy copilot can help you clarify your thinking before you take your potential solution to other members of your executive team or to your Board.

The most effective CEOs I've known in my 25+ years in consulting are the ones who take feedback from three or four different sources before making a decision, and who are not attached to a specific outcome. This allows them to come to the right decision.

As the CEO, you also have to be able to zoom out and consider the broader business strategy that may be at odds with the direction in which a particular division is moving. Even if that division is proving profitable, if it does not align with the overarching company goals, it may need to be dissolved, divested or sold off.

When it comes to ego, you have to understand where your strengths lie. You might be really entrepreneurial and a brilliant startup CEO, but that doesn't mean you have what it takes to stabilise and grow a business that private equity companies will want to invest in.

You have to put your ego to one side, particularly if what you're working on is a passion project, and view it from a more detached perspective. Some of your assumptions might need to be challenged to help you move forward. You need to be able to accept that challenge and welcome it for the good of the organisation.

- **Have the ability to deconstruct situations and reconstruct them rapidly:** I've already talked at various points about the value of having a demolition mindset, and this is very similar. If you think about this in mathematical terms, you're trying to find the common denominator or the

Chapter 16:
The Rise of the Intrapreneur

common baseline in your workflows and processes. Often, you won't find that until you can deconstruct many parts of the business and see them from a higher level.

Many companies prefer to bring in consultants to do this for them, but I believe it is far better to train your leadership team to have a demolition mindset and to give them the time and space to deconstruct business processes and workflows so that they can rebuild them stronger.

Although a CEO can do this on their own, in my experience you achieve the best outcomes when you involve the whole executive team who can all lend their own creativity and unique perspectives to the task.

The people who are most effective at demolishing parts of a business are the ones who are able to see a further horizon than those on their team, and who are happy to build a unit to focus on those opportunities and manage it for a few years to bring the innovation to fruition, before moving on to something new.

Spotlight on Tony Matharu

Role: Founder and Chair of Blue Orchid Hotels

Tenure: July 2019–present

Biggest strengths: Philanthropy, growing businesses, working with community.

Achievements: During the peak of the pandemic in March 2020, Tony launched a hotel chain that he kept open to key workers. In addition, he founded the Central London Alliance (CLA) which invests in and helped London recover post-pandemic by supporting businesses, charities and arts.

Chapter 16:
The Rise of the Intrapreneur

As the owner of a hotel group, Tony Matharu was one of many in the hospitality industry faced with needing to make big decisions about his business very quickly during the Covid-19 pandemic. He knows better than most how one event can change an entire business operation, almost overnight.

When we spoke on the *Between the Lines with Haig* podcast, he explained how he pivoted his operations during the pandemic. In doing so, he demonstrated many of the traits of someone with a fixer mindset. Tony had only just opened his new hotel business, Blue Orchid chain, when the pandemic hit. Instead of shutting his doors and furloughing all the staff, he took a different tack.[43]

> "It seemed really odd to me that at a time when there was a lot of need, hotels chose to close. There were a lot of vulnerable people. There were people who were isolated, others who were stranded, and there were key workers who were working very hard under really challenging circumstances who felt uncomfortable going home having spent shifts working on Covid wards.

---

43   *Between the Lines with Haig*, Tony Matharu (May 2021). Available at: https://www.haigbarrettpartners.com/between-the-lines-with-haig/episode/bc76d141/episode-15-heavenly-view-of-london-with-tony-matharu.

> These people needed local accommodation, sustenance and warmth.
>
> Rather than do what most hotels did, which was to shut the doors, lock up and furlough staff, I tried to do what I could to keep them open. In fact, all of my hotels stayed open during the pandemic and responded to whatever the need was."

But Tony didn't stop with supporting those working in the NHS and those who needed accommodation for other reasons. He realised that London's community as a whole needed support – not just on an individual level, but for the businesses, galleries, museums and other attractions that were all deeply affected by the pandemic.

> "I set up Central London Alliance as a community interest company. We have been able to raise funds with the purpose of helping London and Londoners survive and recover [after the pandemic]. It has picked up huge momentum.
>
> There are now thousands of businesses, and organisations, that are advocates, business supporters or brand partners, connected to this common theme of collaborating and partnering to assist London in getting off its knees and to recover in the best way possible."

Chapter 16:
The Rise of the Intrapreneur

The CLA runs events throughout the year, as well as providing businesses in the UK's capital with resources and various kinds of support to help them thrive. Since starting out, the alliance has launched campaigns to encourage public engagement with central London's offerings, supporting local businesses and cultural institutions in the process.[44]

This is a great example of ecosystem thinking. Tony recognised that by working with other organisations within his community, his business would be stronger. Of course, the businesses he works alongside also benefit from this agreement. This is just one example of how businesses are working smarter following the pandemic.

Creating a win-win economic strategy

William also talked about the approach Haier takes to business, which involves creating win-win economic strategies. This moves the business away from zero-sum thinking (if you win, I have to lose, or vice versa) and allows it to grow through a multitude of opportunities.

He shared an example whereby Haier used its knowledge and understanding of its customers to develop a whole

---

44   Available at: https://www.centrallondonalliance.com/

new business area with the support of carefully selected partners.

> "Here in Thailand (in 2020), GE Appliance worked out an experience service for people who had never had air conditioning before. They found there was an unmet need for people who couldn't afford to buy air conditioning."

Through careful research, Haier discovered many of these people were farmers who would like to have air conditioning, but who couldn't afford the initial outlay for a unit, nor could they get a loan because their income fluctuated too much seasonally. As a result, the company came up with a service whereby they provided the air conditioning unit to the farmers, who could just pay for their usage.

> "This solution required GE Appliance to cooperate with the largest local telecom company, AIS, because this organisation had the connectivity required through its cellular network. GE Appliance put the IoT [internet of things] sensors into the air conditioning units, which could transmit the data about each farmer's usage via AIS' cellular network. That information would then get ported to one of Thailand's largest banks, SCB, which could send the farmer a monthly bill

Chapter 16:
The Rise of the Intrapreneur

based on their usage. The farmer could pay this using their banking app from their home.

The point is GE Appliance didn't have to invest in the network connectivity, they partnered with AIS. They also partnered with the bank to access the infrastructure required to have this solution make sense, be practical and work for the target market that had never been served before.

We're back to humanity. Everybody won. The customer won, and all the partners in the ecosystem won. This gives you an indication of how GE Appliance has been growing at 20 per cent compounded annually."

Ecosystem thinking is a different approach to business and one that can be incredibly powerful. To harness this kind of thinking, we need to move away from a combative approach to business and instead seek collaboration for everyone's benefit wherever possible.

Strategic Copilot
A CEO's Guide to Changing Times

Chapter 17

Changing Ways of Working

There have been many shifts in the way we work over the years, but none have caused such pronounced and immediate change as the Covid-19 pandemic did in 2020. Literally overnight, businesses had to find a way to operate fully remotely. Offices closed. Only those in what were deemed key jobs in the UK were able to go to a physical place of work. Even then, the way in which people worked changed dramatically.

As the world began to open up again following the Covid-19 pandemic, and people started to return to "normal" life, businesses had to grapple with what to do. Should they go back to full-time office-based work?

Should they stay fully remote? Could a hybrid model work better?

In what was termed "the great resignation", record numbers of people left their jobs in 2021, a trend which continued into 2022. The WEF noted that while many were motivated by higher salaries, others cited wanting greater fulfilment from their work as the reason why they sought a new employer.

Interestingly, a significant gap opened up between how employees want to work, and how businesses want people to work. Just 11 per cent of people surveyed want to work full-time in-person, whereas 18 per cent of employers will expect people in the office.[45] Flexibility around work has become increasingly important to many people. The pandemic gave people an opportunity to experience a better work-life balance and resulted in a kind of revolution against the robotic office life, where people spend 9am–5pm in a cubicle.

I saw this through my clients, some of whom could not get their employees back into the office. People were flat-out refusing to travel to an office after having worked from home for over a year. As we have moved further

---

[45] World Economic Forum (2022) "The Great Resignation is not over: Here's what employees say matters most at the workplace". Available at: https://www.weforum.org/stories/2022/06/the-great-resignation-is-not-over/.

Chapter 17:
Changing Ways of Working

away from the pandemic and lockdowns, businesses are increasingly turning to a hybrid model to balance flexibility and freedom for employees with what's required from a business perspective.

There is a general acceptance that commuting five days per week is unnecessary in many jobs, and for many people takes up too much time in their week. Smart businesses are listening to their people and learning to trust that they can be productive from home, while also working out what parts of a role benefit from being carried out in person.

This was a topic I discussed in detail with Alistair Cox, on the *Other Side of the Business Card* podcast. At the time, he was CEO of global recruiter Hays plc and he felt that people had learned a lot from their experiences during the Covid-19 pandemic.[46]

---

46   *Other Side of the Business Card*, Alistair Cox (November 2021). Available at: https://www.haigbarrettpartners.com/the-other-side-of-the-business-card/episode/d2d96a6d/the-power-of-investing-in-yourself-with-alistair-cox-ceo-of-hays-plc.

Spotlight on Alistair Cox

Role: Former Chief Executive of Hays plc

Tenure: 2007–2023

Biggest strengths: Globally minded approach to recruitment, ability to adapt and change within his career. He's pivoted from engineering to management, research science and executive leadership.

Achievements: Heading up a global FTSE 250 firm. Creating a strong company culture while working fully remotely.

Chapter 17:
Changing Ways of Working

"I think that people have appreciated the flexibility that being able to work from home has given them. At Hays, we're probably in a majority of companies who are saying, as we move back into a more normal world (whatever that's going to be), we've got to find that balance between what you do in the office and why you go there.

There are many positives to being in an office, let's be clear about that, but there's no reason we can't give people flexibility around their working hours and working environment if they are productive and getting things done, and this is organised on a planned basis.

The trick is figuring out how to blend the best of what we used to have with the best we've recently had. I'm optimistic that if we get that right, as a society and businesses in general, then we can end up in a much more powerful position with a more engaged, happier, more productive workforce."

From what I've seen, the great resignation that followed the Covid-19 pandemic empowered people who work hard to find a better balance, whether that was to be there more for their kids, to have more downtime at the end of the day or to have more space for other activities. Alongside this empowerment, we've seen people in the younger generation – gen Z – being very clear that work is not just about money. They want a job with purpose, where they're doing something they really enjoy.

Culture is the key

When you're developing a new way of working, or cementing a transition like many businesses have after the pandemic, you need to focus on your work culture, because this will mean the difference between having a productive, engaged workforce and one that takes advantage of more flexible working arrangements in a detrimental way.

In almost every offsite that myself and my team host for leadership teams, the issues they need help with come back to culture. You need to start by having the right people in your leadership team, because they will help develop and maintain the kind of culture you want in your organisation. If you don't invest in your leadership team, that in itself is an indication of your workplace culture. Failing to invest in this area means your leadership team won't be able to propagate the kind of culture you want to see.

William Malek, who you've heard from already in this book, always stresses that every time you bring someone new into your leadership team, you are forming a new

Chapter 17:
Changing Ways of Working

culture. Whether you like it or not, each new person you bring in will subtly shift the culture in your business.

Alistair also identified culture as one of the key drivers of his decisions around how to adapt to the new modes of working following the pandemic.

> "We must have a way of reinforcing, growing and evolving our culture. If everybody's sitting at home, logged on to a system all day, every day, for the rest of their lives, I think your culture starts to evaporate. If you can log into this system, you could easily log into someone else's system for a small pay rise. So we identified a few 'must-haves' around the training and development of not just new recruits, but all of us, because we all need to upskill.
>
> We asked questions like 'how are we going to do that [training] if we don't actually sit in the same room? How are we going to reinforce and grow our culture if we don't sit in the same room?' For me personally, I think innovation and creativity is better when you're sparking with others in the same room. I find it harder to do that through a computer screen – not impossible, but harder.
>
> So when we were talking about what we were going to do with our business, and how we were

going to evolve, we focused on identifying the things that are better when you're in the same room, as well as the things you can easily do, or do better, remotely. We realised we were going to end up with a far more flexible business model. But it was mine and my leadership team's role to set the boundaries within the business that everyone had to work within.

Each individual employee has different challenges, so a one-size-fits-all mandate from the top doesn't work. Instead we have to set the boundaries of what we must cherish and nurture within the business, and create a culture that enables people to design their own systems within those boundaries."

One thing that, for me, has stood out about this shift to more flexible working arrangements is the need for young people to be in an office environment where they can learn from those around them almost by osmosis. This is why a hybrid solution, as far as I see it, is often the best way to go, because when it's implemented in the right way it can deliver the best of both worlds. As we've seen, employees are not going to accept a wholesale return to "old" ways of working, and any executives that fail to grasp that and move with the times will lose talent to their competitors.

Chapter 17:
Changing Ways of Working

Embracing the next technology trend: AI

Another way in which our working environments are changing is through the introduction of AI. Unlike with previous technological inventions, like digital solutions and software for ERP or sales force integration, where the use case was more black and white, the arrival of AI presents new challenges for executive teams. This is technology that will be woven deeper into the fabric of an organisation than anything that has come before.

Executive teams therefore need to understand what role AI should be playing in their business, who it will affect and whose jobs will either be improved or lost as a result of introducing AI.

Education: the best investment in the future

One of the main themes that came out of my conversation with Alistair was the importance of investing in your own education and developing your skills. His story is remarkable. He went from being an aeronautical engineer, to working in the oil and gas industry, to undertaking a self-funded MBA at Stanford University and moving into management and leadership roles.

Educating yourself is one of the best ways you can prepare for new ways of working, as it allows you to pivot into new areas with confidence. Alistair described education as "the underlying foundation of everything in my life" and highlighted how important having a mindset of learning is in today's ever-changing world.

> "You have to get an underlying education and you have to develop a mindset of continually learning, because new things are going to be developed and old things are going to disappear over your working life. I've seen that multiple times and you have to be open-minded about it and not scared of it.
>
> Keep telling yourself, I'll embrace that. I have to learn new things. I'll become something different. I'll reinvent myself. You need that appetite for learning to succeed in this world. You also have to create options and opportunities for yourself and, when they appear, take them."

The value of learning is echoed by another of my Between the Lines with Haig podcast guests, Simon Hocquard, Director General at CANSO, the global voice of air traffic management.[47]

---

47 *Between the Lines with Haig,* Simon Hocquard (March 2021). Available at: https://www.haigbarrettpartners.com/between-the-lines-with-haig/episode/337e1043/episode-5-simon-hocquard-takes-to-the-skies.

Chapter 17:
Changing Ways of Working

Spotlight on Simon Hocquard

Role: Director General, CANSO

Tenure: June 2019–present

Biggest strengths: Ability to lead in a crisis, and his focus on his own wellbeing to allow him to support his team. Extensive experience in career development, leadership, future thinking and innovation.

Achievements: Managing the disruption to air traffic caused by the 2010 volcanic eruption in Iceland; leading CANSO; expanding CANSO's worldwide membership and enhancing the organisation's relationship with industry peers and stakeholders.

Simon also stressed the importance of being able to listen to those around you when you are in a leadership position. Again, this is a shift away from a world in which the CEO is expected to have all the answers.

"I think it's valuable for anyone, certainly someone starting out in their career, to do things you're good at, do things you enjoy, do things you're interested in and to always do things that enable you to learn something new. That could be a skill or a technical competence. You learn things as you have new experiences, and go through leadership and have bigger teams. You often learn how not to do things, as well as how to do things.

I found myself leading the UK operation during the [Icelandic] volcano eruption. There was a huge amount of information available that night. I had a fantastic team of people around me who were very passionate, very knowledgeable and very good at what they did. But as a leader the most important skill is to listen really carefully. At this point, it was all about listening to what people were telling me, and about removing the emotion.

As a leader, as you hear things you make decisions. For me, the key is recognising that you're doing that through filters, which could be your experience, something that's happened

Chapter 17:
Changing Ways of Working

before or your emotions. As a good leader, you have to take a step back, let those filters go and see something for what it is. I remember people becoming very passionate and at times shouting at me during that situation with the volcano, and I had to take my time to really listen and separate fact from fiction. In a crisis, once you've got all the information, then you can make a call.

I was very conscious that I was making some fairly significant decisions. What I found really interesting, which is a testament to how this unfolded, is that after the scenario, the team around me wrote a letter and all signed it to say that they supported every single decision that I made. They acknowledged that it was a very tough ten hours or so through that letter, but for me it was a testament to the importance of taking a step back and listening very carefully as a leader."

One phrase that Simon used during our conversation that really resonated with me was to "listen generously", which he explained means getting rid of all those filters and really focusing on the person in front of you – on what they're thinking and feeling. Simon also stressed the need to listen to truly understand someone else's situation. He pointed out that whether you think what they're saying is real or not, that doesn't change the fact that it's "someone else's reality".

> "You have to listen to really understand that. Then it's not about changing their reality, but about giving them a different context and level of understanding about the situation, and allowing them time (when possible) to develop a new perspective."

To access additional resources around the theme of the new approach to working, scan the following QR code:

Where Do I Start?

There is a lot to digest within this book. You may be wondering how you begin the process of shifting your organisation to be one that welcomes change and is able to pivot within uncertainty. Transformation is a journey, but there is no final destination. Once you have transformed once, you will need to start the cycle over, responding to whatever has shifted in the world around you.

Too many people get stuck on starting. They don't know how to begin, so they don't. Wherever you start your transformation journey, this is much better than not beginning at all. If you stay where you are, your competitors will move around you, and before you know it you will be at the back of the pack.

Within this book, I've shared many tools that can help you to embrace an innovative mindset that is focused on transformation, and tools that can help you bring the rest of your executive team and the rest of the business with you on this journey.

Sometimes it can help to break a longer journey down into shorter sections, so in this final chapter I'll explore what a 100-day strategy plan can look like and explain how it can support you on your first steps along this unpredictable journey of transformation.

Chapter 18

Starting Your Transformation Journey

The world has become more high-stakes and more high-pressure than it ever has been before. Around 10–15 years ago, we saw the rise of big data. But collecting that data is not enough. CEOs need to spend time breaking down and analysing that data, because if they don't, then they will fall behind their competitors.

What makes the world high-stakes is the speed with which transformation occurs and the speed with which information needs to be passed on. The average CEO hasn't seen the companies around them transforming like this before. But while the speed of business and transformation has significantly increased, many of the traditional ways in which CEOs share their strategies, such as through Board meetings, haven't kept up.

This means Boards need to empower their CEOs to act quickly and without the need for constant approval. Similarly, CEOs need to empower their leadership team and others within the organisation to make quick decisions. This makes everything about running a business higher stakes.

To empower your executives in this way, you need to have a clear idea of your strategy, the risks and what your competitors are doing. This is why communication is such a crucial skill to master, because in today's world information is flowing so quickly that you have less time to communicate what's going on, while also having more information to pass on in these interactions.

Why don't people start?

In my experience, the biggest obstacle to "Where do I start?" seems to be that if you don't know exactly what to do, you're not going to start at all. The thing that sets high-performing executives apart is that as long as they have a strategy, they are always going to start, even if they are unsure in some way.

Chapter 18:
Starting Your Transformation Journey

I have lost count of how many times I've heard people say, "I'll start in two months" or "We'll know in three months ..." – pushing decisions further down the line does nothing to help your business innovate and grow. In fact, it means you are likely to miss opportunities to get ahead of your competitors and achieve step-out growth.

Overcoming analysis paralysis

As a CEO you have to accept that uncertainty will always exist, particularly in the world in which we live today. The trick to overcoming analysis paralysis and the desire to wait for greater certainty is to become less uncertain in your actions than your next competitor.

You need to make decisions to the best of your ability, and often that will be helped by taking the time to really dig into your data and to do so in a collaborative way with other members of your team. But, of course, time is often in short supply for executives, and this is where I see technology like AI being incredibly valuable. By using AI to analyse the data about your supply chain, for example, you could give yourself a bit more certainty than your competitors have, and even just one per cent more certainty could be the difference between you getting ahead and falling behind.

Strategic Copilot
A CEO's Guide to Changing Times

Every CEO needs to understand that living long term with uncertainty at what feels like an unmanageable level is not really an option. Instead, you may need more people on the ground internally to help you understand your market better. Or you may need to bring in outside help, whether that's the kind of strategist I've talked about already or bringing new people on to your advisory Board.

The point is, by getting more people from different places involved, you are developing the multiperspectivity that is so crucial for your company's survival and success in the modern world.

Bringing in advisers who aren't part of a consultancy is a new way of working, and one that I encourage my clients to embrace. You can bring in contractors to provide very specific advice at all levels. However, when it comes to leadership teams, I recommend taking a hybrid approach whereby you have strategic advisers who are on hand and can act as part of your executive team when needed.

We have moved away from a world where you would spend two years working with a consultant to complete a strategy project. In the 2020s, the emphasis is on high-impact projects, where you might bring in a consultant for six weeks to help you solve a specific leadership issue or to work out what you need to enter a specific market.

Chapter 18:
Starting Your Transformation Journey

Another option could be to bring someone in on an executive level just one day per week to fill a gap in your executive team. In some cases that might be a specific gap in knowledge, in others it might be to ensure you always have an external perspective to challenge biases and see blind spots. The latter is particularly relevant if your executive team has worked together for a number of years and reached a point where they have a harmonised perspective.

Often, this harmonised perspective can cascade down to those coming through behind the executive leadership team, which can make it hard to find someone internally who is willing to take shots at the strategy and potentially help demolish it.

This again highlights the importance of working with an external expert to help you facilitate those discussions, to give people throughout an organisation an opportunity to take shots at the strategy and business processes, and to evaluate whether what you are doing is still relevant and effective in today's world.

You have to be prepared to change and realign your strategy constantly, because the world is shifting and changing around us. This means you, and the rest of your executive team, need to be open to challenge and willing to discuss potential issues.

In many companies, what is missing is the analysis required to understand the cost of maintaining the status quo. This is one of the elements that an experienced external adviser can bring to the table.

The time is now

The best time to start anything is now. As a leader, if you say that you want to do something within your company, you need to start now. Your start might be conservative, but at least you are making progress in the direction you've chosen. This is the secret to success in today's world. You can't afford to wait for the ideal time, because there's no such thing.

You have to move forward with as much certainty as you can, and you have to learn along the way. The same goes for the members of your leadership team and those coming through behind them. As CEO, you need to empower them to make decisions and you need to know your executives well enough to trust that they're going to make the best decisions they can, within the guardrails you put in place.

Chapter 18:
Starting Your Transformation Journey

Managing (un)certainty

Managing uncertainty comes down to analysing key areas of your business and addressing their unique needs.

When showing clients how to manage uncertainty, we use a framework designed to help business leaders and executives navigate complex challenges and make informed decisions during uncertain times. The framework breaks down the key focus areas required for strategic success – strategic foresight, managing innovation, marketing agility, operating performance and M&A – into actionable insights.

The framework can be illustrated as a mindmap where each branch outlines common challenges and corresponding actions that leaders can take to build resilience, strengthen their operations and seize opportunities. The visual format allows you to quickly identify potential pain points and develop a roadmap for addressing them.

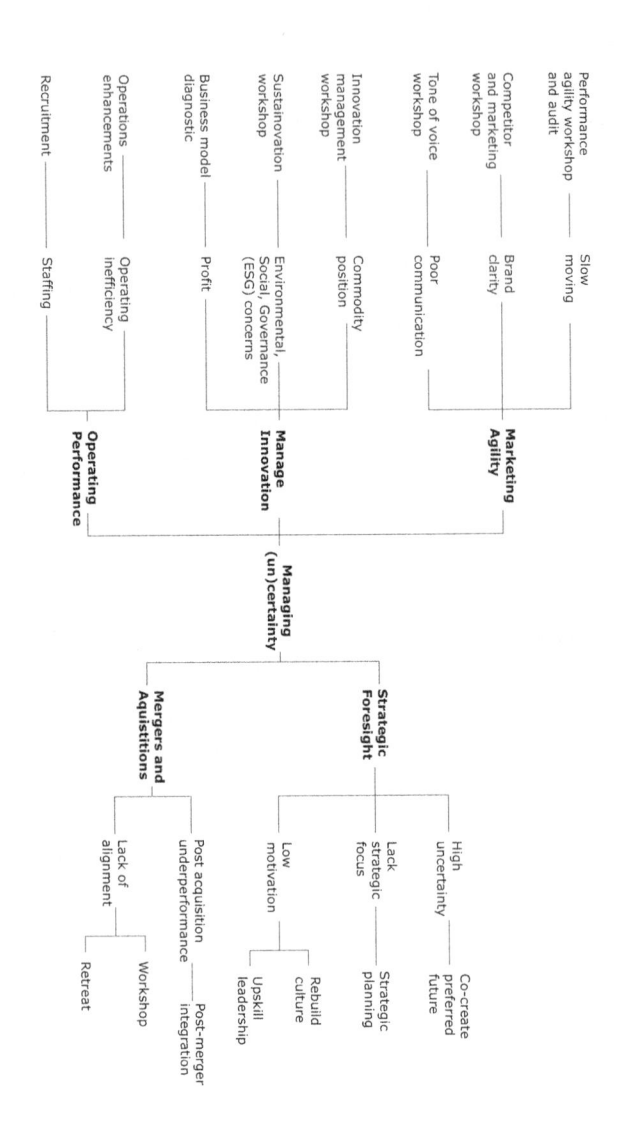

Strategic Copilot
A CEO's Guide to Changing Times

- Performance agility workshop and audit — Slow moving ⎤
- Competitor and marketing workshop — Brand clarity ⎥ **Marketing Agility**
- Tone of voice workshop — Poor communication ⎦

- Innovation management workshop — Commodity position ⎤
- Sustainovation workshop — Environmental, Social, Governance (ESG) concerns ⎥ **Manage Innovation**
- Business model diagnostic — Profit ⎦

- Operations enhancements — Operating inefficiency ⎤ **Operating Performance**
- Recruitment — Staffing ⎦

All feeding into: **Managing (un)Certainty**

- ⎡ Lack of alignment — Workshop ⎤ **Mergers and Aquistitions**
- ⎣ Post acquisition underperformance — Post-merger integration ⎦
   — Retreat

- Low motivation — Upskill leadership ⎤
- Lack strategic focus — Rebuild culture ⎥ **Strategic Foresight**
- High uncertainty — Strategic planning ⎥
- Co-create preferred future ⎦

292

Chapter 18:
Starting Your Transformation Journey

Embrace your inner entrepreneur

Entrepreneurs understand that the rules of yesterday are not necessarily the rules of today, and nor will they be the rules of tomorrow. Two centuries ago, the most effective form of transport was a horse-drawn carriage. Then the automobile was invented with a petrol engine. Now we have hybrid and electric vehicles.

With each evolution the rules have changed and we've already seen the advantage that Toyota developed by being one of the first automakers to move into the hybrid space.

The rules that are in place now are not intended to be there forever. Entrepreneurs are very good at recognising that it is in breaking those rules or in the formation of new rules, that industry breakthroughs occur. As a CEO of a large company, you need to develop your entrepreneurial spirit and encourage a culture of intrapreneurship to break and work with new rules to your advantage.

There is no right or wrong way to do this. The level of risk you're comfortable taking will vary depending on you as an individual, as well as on the business you lead and the industry in which you operate.

For example, a pharmaceutical company will need someone heading it up who can follow rules, because there are strict regulations in place in the sector for good reason. However, in this case you may want to put someone with that intrapreneurial mindset at the head of your protein engineering division where they might be able to identify a new way of doing things that benefits the whole medical community, and by association also humanity.

Whether you are higher or lower risk matters less than being able to communicate the boundaries of risk-taking that are acceptable within different business units to help you stay ahead.

Create a 100-day strategy plan

Creating a 100-day strategy plan enables you to probe and challenge the people in your team to confirm aspects of the general corporate strategy. It also gives you an opportunity to demolish the existing strategy by asking questions rooted in the core philosophy of: "If we broke all of this down, how could we rebuild it?"

You can use the exercise of creating a 100-day strategy plan, or in some cases this might be a 25-day plan depending on your industry, to work with people in adjacent divisions to map every part of the business out and ideally to put all

Chapter 18:
Starting Your Transformation Journey

of this down on paper. Creating a visual roadmap can also be helpful to articulate your thinking and communicate the plan with others in the business.

In Chapter 5 I shared the strategy diamond model with you, which is a collection of the five elements that make up a coherent business strategy. I had the fortune of studying under Donald Hambrick during one of the many executive education courses I completed at Columbia Business School in the late 1990s. Use this as the basis for creating your 100-day strategy plan and work through the three Cs analysis – company, competition, customer – followed by exploring the environment you operate in, both in the short and long term.

This allows you to map out the strategy, the arenas you play in and how you're going to get there, which covers your core capabilities and competencies. Once you have the strategy mapped out, you can agree on timings for each component and that will give you the clarity you need to create an implementation plan. An implementation plan provides you with the structure you need around the people involved, the information systems and so on. This is the practical side of your strategy.

We don't move forward with any client that doesn't have their strategy diamond mapped out because we know that when this is done correctly, it makes a strategy much more likely to succeed.

Case study: The strategy diamond in practice

A mid-sized US financial services company approached us at a pivotal moment when external market pressures and internal inefficiencies were limiting its ability to scale and innovate.

Challenges identified

Through our strategic analysis, we uncovered several key challenges:

- **Siloed functions:** Departments operated independently, leading to duplicated efforts and inconsistent client experiences.
- **Reactive decision-making:** The organisation's response to market changes was often delayed due to the absence of an integrated strategy.
- **Employee misalignment:** The team lacked a unified understanding of priorities, which affected productivity and employee engagement.

Applying the strategy diamond

1. Defining the arenas (where to compete)

We collaborated with the leadership team to identify the most critical service categories and market segments.

Chapter 18:
Starting Your Transformation Journey

The focus areas included high-growth industries, such as fintech startups and family-owned businesses requiring tailored financial services. A geographic analysis helped identify new office locations where client demand was increasing.

2. Building competitive advantage (how to win)

The firm's unique strength in providing personalised advisory services was highlighted as a key differentiator.

A refined value proposition focused on "responsiveness and innovation", which meant leveraging technology to provide faster and more insightful financial reporting.

A cross-departmental collaboration framework was introduced to break down silos and foster knowledge sharing.

3. Developing capabilities (what's needed to succeed)

A comprehensive talent review led to tailored training programmes and a clearer structure for employee growth.

Investments in cloud-based accounting software and data integration tools improved workflows and enhanced client reporting. Key operational improvements included a "one-stop service" intake process, reducing onboarding time by 30 per cent.

4. Sequencing and implementation (how to get there)

We created an implementation roadmap with clear milestones for strategy rollout. Weekly alignment meetings and monthly check-ins ensured accountability and continuous feedback.

Leaders were equipped with dashboards to track performance metrics and make real-time adjustments.

Results

Within 12 months, the company experienced measurable improvements:

- A 25 per cent increase in annual revenue due to stronger client retention and service expansion.
- Internal workflows became more streamlined, reducing manual tasks by 40 per cent.
- The percentage of employees reporting alignment with the organisation's vision increased by 50 per cent.
- The company expanded into two new geographic regions, strengthening its brand recognition in key markets.

These results demonstrate the power of following the strategy diamond model. By gaining clarity over where they were competing, how they could win, what was

Chapter 18:
Starting Your Transformation Journey

needed to succeed and how to get there, the organisation in question was able to solve all the key challenges we identified when we started working with them and expanded its operations.

To access additional resources to help you start to develop a strategy fit for the modern world, scan the following QR code:

Strategic Copilot
A CEO's Guide to Changing Times

Confidence in Uncertainty

Every CEO wants to move forward with their team with clarity, focus and peace of mind. A key element of moving forward in uncertainty is keeping yourself and your leadership team ahead of the future.

There are a multitude of things that affect a business and its future ability to perform:

- Divestiture
- Mergers and acquisitions
- New crisis response systems
- Innovation
- Sustainability
- Customer loyalty

- Leadership team

All of these elements have the ability to lift you up or drag you down. As your business becomes more complex and challenging, your business plan becomes a game of snakes and ladders. You encounter many setbacks around every corner (snakes). But if you make the right decisions you have the opportunity to significantly accelerate your growth and performance (ladders).

There are three main themes that allow you to identify the ladders and successfully climb them:

1. Managing risk.

2. Creating and leveraging opportunity.

3. Building strategic focus around a structured transformation.

Managing risk

Taking everything we've talked about in this book, you have to manage risk by future-proofing your organisation. Today's business environment is influenced by extremes which means your advanced planning and strategic foresight is critical. Extreme changes can be categorised by industries, technologies and regions of the world, which include:

Global changes

- The successful emergence of the Middle East as a global player in business has created immense opportunities. The region is now a hub for innovation, investment and partnerships, particularly in industries such as energy, technology and construction. Businesses operating globally must adapt their strategies to engage with this influential market.
- Emerging markets in Africa, south-east Asia and Latin America are experiencing rapid digitalisation, creating tech-driven growth in previously untapped regions. These developments open the door to new consumers, innovative business models and the potential for companies to expand their reach globally while contributing to infrastructure and technological development.

Biotechnology industry

- Innovations, such as personalised medicine and gene-editing tools like CRISPR, are creating entirely new markets and opportunities for businesses, from pharmaceuticals to healthcare technology providers. As an example, personalised medicine enables treatments that are tailored to individual patients, increasing their effectiveness and driving demand for more specialised healthcare products.

- Advances in telemedicine are also transforming how healthcare services are delivered, breaking down geographical barriers and enabling companies to provide care to previously underserved populations. Businesses that invest in these technologies stand to capture significant market share in the rapidly evolving biotech landscape.
- Breakthroughs in vaccine technology, particularly mRNA vaccines, have revolutionised the speed and scalability of vaccine production, presenting new business opportunities across the pharmaceutical supply chain.

Construction industry

- Digital twins and Building Information Modelling (BIM) technology allow teams to create detailed, interactive models of projects before breaking ground. These tools reduce errors, improve collaboration and optimise costs throughout the project life cycle.
- 3D printing in construction is another gamechanger, allowing for faster build times, reduced material waste and significant cost savings. This technology is particularly impactful

in addressing housing shortages, as it enables the construction of affordable homes at scale.
- Sustainable building materials, such as carbon-neutral concrete and self-healing concrete, are not only reducing the environmental impact of construction but also offering competitive advantages to companies adopting these innovations. As demand for green buildings rises, construction firms leveraging these materials can differentiate themselves in the market.
- Robotics and automation, including robotic bricklayers and drones for surveying, are further improving efficiency, safety and precision in construction projects. Companies that embrace these technologies are positioned to lead in a highly competitive industry.

Oil and gas industry

- Advances in carbon capture, utilisation and storage (CCUS) technology allow companies to capture CO_2 emissions from industrial processes and either store it underground or repurpose it for other uses. This positions oil and gas companies as leaders in the global energy transition while meeting stricter emissions targets.
- The development of technology enabling hydrogen as an alternative fuel is creating new revenue streams for oil and gas companies. Hydrogen

is gaining traction as a clean energy source, particularly for hard-to-electrify sectors like heavy industry and transportation.
- AI-driven enhanced oil recovery (EOR) techniques optimise extraction processes, increasing production from existing wells while reducing exploration costs. Companies leveraging this technology can extend the life of their assets.
- IoT-enabled monitoring systems and digital oilfields provide real-time data on equipment performance, production levels and safety. These technologies improve operational efficiency and reduce downtime, lowering costs significantly.
- Oil and gas companies are diversifying into offshore wind energy, leveraging their knowledge in offshore operations to build renewable energy portfolios. This allows them to balance traditional operations with green initiatives.
- Improved seismic-imaging technologies allow more accurate identification of oil and gas reserves, reducing risks and costs in exploration while improving the success rate of drilling operations.
- Investments in biofuel technology, such as converting waste into renewable diesel, offer a sustainable alternative to traditional petroleum products and diversify revenue streams.

Mining industry

- Automated vehicles and robotic mining equipment are increasing efficiency and reducing risks in hazardous environments. These technologies allow companies to operate 24/7, cut labour costs and improve safety for workers.
- AI-driven tools are helping companies analyse vast amounts of geological data to identify optimal mining sites more accurately and cost-effectively. Predictive analytics also enable proactive maintenance of equipment, reducing downtime and improving operational efficiency.
- Sustainable mining practices, such as the adoption of electric mining equipment and renewable energy sources, are helping companies reduce their environmental footprint. These efforts align with global environmental, social and governance (ESG) expectations, improving reputational and regulatory outcomes.
- Urban mining involves extracting valuable metals and minerals from electronic waste, creating a new and sustainable revenue stream for mining companies. The practice addresses resource scarcity while contributing to the circular economy.
- Water and waste management technologies are becoming essential in regions with scarce resources. These innovations not only enhance

sustainability but also help companies manage costs and regulatory pressures.
- The growing demand for critical minerals like lithium, cobalt and rare earth elements, driven by the EV and renewable energy industries, is creating opportunities for mining companies to expand into high-growth sectors.

Automotive industry

- The global shift towards EVs is revolutionising the automotive sector. Companies are investing heavily in battery technology, charging infrastructure and new manufacturing processes to meet the rising demand for sustainable transportation. EV adoption is also driving partnerships with renewable energy providers.
- Advances in autonomous driving technology are transforming how consumers think about transportation. Self-driving vehicles are creating opportunities in ride-hailing services, logistics and urban planning, while challenging traditional manufacturers to innovate or risk falling behind.
- IoT-enabled vehicles provide real-time data on driving behaviour, vehicle performance and traffic conditions. This connectivity allows automakers to offer subscription-based services, enhancing revenue streams while improving customer experiences.

- The use of advanced lightweight and sustainable materials like carbon fibre composites and recycled metals is improving fuel efficiency and reducing the environmental impact of vehicle production. Companies adopting these materials gain a competitive edge in sustainability-conscious markets.
- The rise of mobility as a service (MaaS) platforms, combining public and private transport options into seamless, app-based experiences, is disrupting car ownership models. Automotive companies are adapting by offering subscription or pay-per-use services.
- Hydrogen-powered vehicles are emerging as an alternative to EVs, particularly in heavy-duty applications like trucks and buses. This diversification offers opportunities for companies to target niche markets and expand beyond traditional offerings.
- The rise of shared mobility services, such as carpooling and micromobility (e.g. scooters and bikes), is changing consumer preferences. Automotive companies are diversifying their offerings to cater to these new trends.
- Companies are embracing circular manufacturing practices, recycling end-of-life vehicles and reusing materials to minimise waste and reduce production costs. This approach not only supports

sustainability, but also aligns with shifting consumer and regulatory expectations.

Managing risk effectively requires you to be aware of the extreme changes that are possible, or already occurring, in your industry. This means developing your future thinking around threat scenarios, situation assessments, effective scanning of weak signals and strategic foresight to help your company determine its current level of resilience to known and unknown risks.

You have to anticipate the uncertainty, and in doing so you will give yourself and your organisation confidence in uncertainty. To have confidence you need certain mechanisms in place to support you and your decision-making, such as determining likely risk triggers and protection points, and developing full-term scenarios. This will give you a plan B to deploy your major assets, personnel, product and business operations, cash reserves and so on.

The third part of managing risk involves anchoring your business. Disruptive change may have a negative impact on your business, so put in place whatever steps you need to in order to shield your operation from negative disruptive change and ensure that your minimum viable business model is always protected.

Creating and leveraging opportunity

This is the flip side of managing risk. Do you have the ability to create opportunity? The more your business makes an investment in facing internal and external threats that you see ahead, the more you will find real advantages to streamline, focus and grow your current business.

Analysis is the key to action. It's important to look into these areas, and if you don't have the tools within your executive team to do so, then bring in an external firm or consultant who can support you to look at analysis, industry shifts and business models. Doing so will provide you with a fresh look at new opportunities for you to make the most of discipline and cycle planning for today, as well as the future.

When it comes to leveraging the opportunities you create, strategy demands excellence in all phases of implementation. It requires special focus if you are to embark on step-change growth and high-risk transformation projects, as set out in the following initiatives:

- **A culture reset:** This is particularly important if you're going through changes in employee working styles – for a remote-hybrid reset if your organisation is now more global; or a shift to more local working because of supply chain risk, for example.

- **Customer loyalty:** You have access to a lot of big data and are ideally at the level of incorporating AI to help you better understand customer trends and how you can better serve your customers.
- **Digital transformation:** Ideally, your digital transformation will be complete, but if you haven't started, then you need to. Or you might be moving into the next phase of your digital transformation if it's an incremental process.
- **Mergers and acquisitions:** Although organic growth is often the best idea, M&A activity tends to be a quick fix. The key is to ask whether it's going to improve your economies of scale, increase your market share distribution or enhance your financial resources. The bottom line is, only explore M&A activity that will bring long-term value.
- **Sustainovation:** In 2011 I had a sustainability division in my consultancy where we coined the term "sustainovation" (a combination of sustainability and innovation). We would hold workshops to demonstrate to companies how sustainability can drive innovation and result in a competitive advantage for businesses in any sector.

Patagonia are an example of a company that aligns with the principles of sustainovation, including:

- **Executive intent:** Their founder Yvon Chouinard set sustainability as a core priority and built initiatives like 1% for the Planet. In 2022, Yvon and the rest of the Chouinard family took the extraordinary step of making planet Earth the company's only shareholder. All profit that is not reinvested in the business itself is put towards protecting the planet, through the Patagonia Purpose Trust. It's an incredibly innovative approach to operating sustainably within the capitalist system.
- **Storytelling:** Patagonia makes a strong investment into impactful marketing campaigns including short films and social media initiatives that tell their sustainability story.
- **Continuous learning:** The company regularly introduces experimental pilots (such as biofabricated materials) to push sustainable product innovation further.

You can find more information on sustainovation, and read our white paper on the subject, on our resources page, which can be accessed via the QR codes in this book.

Building strategic focus around a structured transformation

To meet the challenges in the current marketplace, your company needs to engage in deeper, more systematic organisational change or seek a different approach to operational management. This is where the strategic planning alternatives we've discussed in this book will be useful.

This process is all about reshaping your culture, disrupting your thinking and then growing through innovation. Many companies want to innovate, but they get stuck for a multitude of reasons.

By answering the key questions that follow, you can start to build your own blueprint for success. It is important to reiterate here the value of bringing in an external perspective. Creating the blueprint for action is a starting point to help our clients prioritise their resources given the range of potential global futures.

Blueprint for success

A successful transformation begins with creating a blueprint for action. This is a clear, prioritised plan that allocates resources effectively and adapts to a range of future scenarios. This blueprint should focus on three key pillars:

1. Risk management

2. Opportunity leverage

3. Strategic focus

For each pillar, you can ask targeted questions to assess where your organisation stands and identify areas for improvement.

1. Managing risk

Assess your organisation's ability to anticipate, mitigate and respond to risks:

- Does your leadership team have a clear vision that guides decision-making during crises?
- Is your business resilient enough to withstand unexpected challenges?
- Have you reanalysed your processes to reduce costs and maximise profit margins without sacrificing long-term growth?
- Can your organisation survive and thrive when severely challenged?

- Do you have systems in place to notify management of quality or process issues early?

2. Leveraging opportunities

Examine how well your organisation identifies and capitalises on new opportunities:

- Are you prioritising the right business processes to reach your preferred future?
- Does your executive team have the capacity and expertise to lead innovation initiatives?
- Have you created new markets or value networks that differentiate your business?
- Are you investing enough in R&D to gain a competitive advantage?
- Do you regularly assess and refine business processes to ensure they remain fit for purpose?

3. Building strategic focus

Evaluate whether your organisation has the clarity and discipline to execute its strategy effectively:

- Do your current objectives align with your long-term vision?

- Have roles, responsibilities and procedures been clearly defined across the organisation?
- Do you have frameworks or tools in place to guide decision-making during periods of uncertainty?
- Is your senior leadership team prioritising projects to respond to multiple future scenarios?
- Are you maintaining a structured and rigorous approach to managing critical systems?

Embedding disruptive innovation

Disruptive innovation requires organisations to be prepared for radical change:

- Is your company ready to explore entirely new directions?
- Do you have focus models that help you navigate complexity and find emerging opportunities?
- Does your leadership team have the skills and resilience to guide the organisation through disruption?

Innovation isn't just about creating new products – it's about rethinking how your organisation creates value and adapts to shifting market demands. Success comes from fostering a culture where experimentation, agility and learning are embedded at every level.

Final thoughts

Building strategic focus is an ongoing process that requires both reflection and bold action. By addressing risk, seizing opportunities and maintaining clarity of purpose, you can position your organisation not only to survive future disruptions but to thrive because of them.

To ensure long-term success, don't hesitate to seek external perspectives. A fresh set of eyes can challenge assumptions, uncover blind spots and help your leadership team move forward with confidence.

Transformation is a journey, not a one-off project. The best time to start is now. Because waiting for the perfect moment may mean missing it entirely.

About the Author

Haig Armaghanian is a business leader, thought leader and podcaster with a keen sense for creating and maintaining strategic advantage for his clients. Challenging the status quo of an ever-evolving corporate playing field, he shakes things up with his disruptive thinking – looking at organisations through a different lens; supporting them to make the changes necessary to remain relevant and turn uncertainty into innovation during uncertain times.

Strategic Copilot
A CEO's Guide to Changing Times

Born and raised in the UK, Haig earned a Bachelor of Science (Honours) in Chemical Engineering from the University of Surrey. While working in business, Haig has completed several senior executive educational courses from establishments including Columbia Business School, University of Michigan and UCLA. Haig has lived in France, Belgium and the USA for the past 25+ years, and recently relocated back to London, England.

He strives to bring the necessary perspective, people, experience and proven methodology to help his clients lead their organisations, manage their teams and prioritise resources in a "black swan" world. After 12 years in leading management roles at Rio Tinto, Haig began his entrepreneurial journey in consulting which, over the past 25 years, has seen him work in four continents, 30 countries and on over 200 projects.

Haig's consulting background includes specialising in innovation, new product/service development, business models, marketing strategy, family businesses and leveraging branding work to drive people, culture and performance.

When not working, Haig enjoys a good peaty Lagavulin 16 and a fine Cuban cigar, balanced with a regular dose of yoga. He's a keen cook – French and Armenian dishes are his specialities – and he marvels daily at what his two young daughters discover.

Strategic Copilot
A CEO's Guide to Changing Times

Printed in Great Britain
by Amazon